Jacques Rivière

Twayne's World Authors Series

Maxwell A. Smith, Editor of French Literature

Professor Emeritus, The University of Chattanooga

Former Visiting Professor in Modern Languages,
The Florida State University

TWAS 633

JACQUES RIVIÈRE
(1886–1925)

Sketch by Deanna Stefanek from a
photograph which appeared in *Quelques progrès dans l'étude du coeur humain
(Freud et Proust)*

Jacques Rivière

By Karen D. Levy

University of Tennessee, Knoxville

Twayne Publishers • Boston

Jacques Rivière

Karen D. Levy

Copyright © 1982 by G. K. Hall & Company
All Rights Reserved
Published by Twayne Publishers
A Division of G. K. Hall & Company
70 Lincoln Street
Boston, Massachusetts 02111

Book production by Marne B. Sultz

Book design by Barbara Anderson

Printed on permanent/durable acid-free
paper and bound in the United States of
America.

Library of Congress Cataloging in Publication Data

Levy, Karen D.
 Jacques Rivière.

 (Twayne's world authors series ; TWAS 633)
 Bibliography: p. 170
 Includes index.
  1. Rivière, Jacques, 1886–1925.   2. Authors, French—
20th century—Biography.   I. Title.   II. Series.
PQ2635.I87Z76   848'.91209 [B]   82-6056
ISBN O-8057-6476-3   AACR2

Contents

About the Author

Karen D. Levy did her undergraduate work at Ursuline College for Women in Cleveland, Ohio, and her doctoral studies at the University of Kentucky, specializing in twentieth-century French literature. She is an associate professor in the Department of Romance Languages at the University of Tennessee, Knoxville.

Preface

Any attempt to present a fair and accurate assessment of Jacques Rivière's career is an extremely complicated problem because of the varied nature of his writings and his relationship with some of the towering literary figures of early twentieth-century France, such as Paul Claudel, André Gide, and Marcel Proust. It will be our task to define each of Rivière's many interests and discuss their significance in the pattern of his overall development. But it is important to note at the very beginning that Rivière was first and foremost a critic who, after World War I, became the guiding force behind the most prestigious French literary review of his time and an astute political observer as well.

In the late nineteenth and early twentieth centuries, French criticism was dominated by two different methods. It was influenced, on the one hand, by the positivistic theories of Hippolyte Taine and, on the other, by the basically biographical approach of Sainte-Beuve. Taine treated literary creations as products to be classified according to scientific criteria, while Sainte-Beuve was mainly interested in presenting detailed portraits of authors and viewed their works in direct relation to external circumstances.[1] Rivière was among the first of his generation to react against the extremes of both of these methods and to stress the primary importance of the work itself in formulating critical evaluations. He was one of the earliest twentieth-century French writers to consider criticism as an intense personal experience of interaction with the intricacies of the text and with the consciousness of the author as manifested in it. He based his judgments on the evidence he found in the language, style, and overall structure of the works being treated. As we shall see with regard to his studies of Claudel, Gide, and Proust, Rivière's reaction sprang from direct contact with their works. He would use biographical or historical information to enhance his remarks or to develop his points in a broader perspective, but it was the literary texts themselves which were the source of all his evaluations.

Much of Rivière's critical legacy consists of the personal essays and the numerous studies of authors, painters, and composers which appeared in the distinguished *Nouvelle Revue Française,* founded in 1909 and still in existence today. Rivière started to contribute to the journal almost immediately after it began to appear. In 1911 he became the *NRF*'s secretary, and from 1919 until his death in 1925 he served as its director. When he was in charge of the review, Rivière continually emphasized the necessity for literary excellence coupled with open-mindedness and defended these principles in the face of, at times, overwhelming opposition.

In the fall of 1924, for example, he spoke out vehemently against the extremely reactionary Catholic critic Henri Massis, who had recently accused the *NRF* of moral laxity and denounced the influence of André Gide. Rivière published an open letter to Massis in October in which he condemned his correspondent's didacticism, clarified once and for all the role which Gide had actually played in the lives of those young Frenchmen who came to maturity in the early years of the twentieth century, and also summed up what could be considered the constants in his own evolution.[2] In replying to Massis's rigid, moralistic directive that a novelist must forcibly choose between depicting good or evil and instruct his reader through his work, Rivière insisted that "There is also something which advances toward you . . . one begins by no longer recognizing at all what one is seeing: it is life, at this moment, one who is gifted as a novelist feels an enormous [sense of] caution overwhelm him. He sees beings quite near to him who are living, who are moving, and he thinks: first of all understand them, first of all depict them."[3] An author must be committed to the adventure of living and writing and hence be open to all experiences. He must be willing to go wherever his characters lead him and explore all options open to him without prejudice if his work is to be authentic.

This statement concerning the intrinsic value of all human possibilities was the point of departure for Rivière's search for his own identity and his effort to seize and decipher the wholeness of his being in relation to the world around him. It is precisely this general effort "to become oneself" (*NE,* 231) and, in his own case, to develop each of his natural abilities to the fullest, while trying to understand how they functioned within him, which could be said to structure both his life and his approach to literature. Rivière was always seeking to know himself better and to progress further with the knowledge that he gained through introspection, through interaction with the exterior world, or through exposure to different kinds of artistic creation.

During the past fifty years a rather large number of books and articles have been published which deal with Rivière's life and works. Some of them reveal a specifically spiritual orientation. For example, Michel Suffran's enthusiastic book describes Rivière's life in the context of religious conversion, and Bradford Cook's thoughtful study examines the specific way in which Rivière's personal essays, novels, and critical writings manifest the changes in his spiritual evolution. Other critical works, such as the articles written by Rivière's Swiss friends or the recent study by the distinguished critic Marcel Raymond, concentrate on specific aspects of Rivière's critical repertoire. Raymond's penetrating analysis, for example, deals in particular with the significance of those of Rivière's articles that were published under the titles *Etudes* and *Nouvelles Etudes.*

Still other works cover the entire span of Rivière's life and career from a more all-inclusive point of view. They attempt to treat all of Rivière's major concerns and emphasize the broadness of his interests. Martin Turnell's monograph cogently summarizes the major steps in Rivière's personal evolution as well as his literary development. Paul Beaulieu's sensitive study presents a more detailed and more in-depth picture of Rivière's career than Turnell's text. Helen Naughton's illuminating and well-documented analysis provides invaluable biographical information, delves into the intricacies of Rivière's evolution, and clarifies many of the paradoxes surrounding his career as a whole.

Yet even in each of these very worthwhile studies there is still some important area of Rivière's career that is either glossed over or left completely untouched. None of these works, for example, treats in sufficient detail the multi-leveled significance of his voluminous war notebooks, the importance of his experiences in Switzerland in 1917–1918, or the truly modern quality of his contribution to literature and to the *NRF*. These are a few of the areas that need further development and elaboration so that our appreciation for the scope of Rivière's understanding and our insight into the complexity of his attitudes can become clearer and even more precise.

In this study we shall make every effort to follow Rivière's own approach to literature and criticism, attempting to examine his works as honestly and openly as he strove to treat either the works of others or the products of his own creative or critical inspiration. Above all we shall try to avoid being guilty of the criticism which Rivière's Swiss friend André Rivier made concerning the numerous commentaries written on Rivière after his death, all of which revealed "the common trait of trying to reduce, explain, classify, to the detriment of the accuracy of the portrait. . . ."[4] For us, as for Rivière's friend, "One thing alone counts; it is a question of restoring the whole person of Rivière in his exact dimensions and his true complexity."[5]

Perhaps the simplest, most effective way to organize our investigation of Rivière's complexity is to follow a basically chronological approach and to use his vast published correspondence and war diaries, which span the entire twenty years of his career, as a framework in which to situate his extremely varied critical works. By examining and carefully charting the delicate interplay between Rivière's often very intimate personal writings, beginning with the exchanges between him and Fournier, and his vast repertoire of critical publications, we shall be able to follow and to understand fully the evolution of his thought process. By adopting this approach, we hope to reveal the depth of his intellectual curiosity, the accuracy of his comprehension, the significance of his critical method, and the force of his impact on French letters as director of the *NRF*.

Preface

I would like to express my sincere thanks to my colleague Professor Carl Cobb for his invaluable editorial assistance in the preparation of this manuscript.

Karen D. Levy

University of Tennessee, Knoxville

Chronology

1886   15 July, birth of Jacques Rivière in Bordeaux, son of a professor of obstetrics at the University of Bordeaux.

1896   Death of Rivière's mother, Reine Fernaud Rivière, to whom he was very closely attached.

1903   Meeting with Henri Alain-Fournier at the Lycée Lakanal in Paris. Gradually became intimate friends.

1906–1907   Rivière spent a year of military service garrisoned near Bordeaux, finding enough time to continue his university studies in Bordeaux. February 1907, first letter to Paul Claudel expressing his metaphysical anguish and asking for Claudel's counsel. Publication of Rivière's three-part study of Paul Claudel's early plays entitled "Paul Claudel, Poète Chrétien" in the review *L'Occident*.

1908–1909   Founding of the *Nouvelle Revue Française (NRF)*, welcoming new ideas and authors, under the inspiration of André Gide and the editorial direction of Jean Schlumberger, Henri Ghéon, and Jacques Copeau. Rivière met Gide in December 1908, immediately gained his respect, and soon began to contribute regularly to the new review. Rivière failed his exams for the *agrégation* in August 1909. At this time he married Isabelle Fournier, the sister of his best friend, and struggled to eke out a meager living by tutoring in philosophy while, at the same time, continuing with his literary activities for the *NRF*. November 1909, publication of Rivière's first important contribution to the *NRF* entitled "Introduction à une Métaphysique du rêve."

1911   In August, Rivière became the father of a daughter, Jacqueline; in December, he accepted the important position of secretary for the *NRF*. Publication of Rivière's two-part study "André Gide" in *La Grande Revue* and his critical anthology *Etudes*.

1913   Publication of Rivière's analysis of the evolution of the novel, "Le Roman d'aventure," and his article on Stravinsky, *"Le Sacre du printemps."* At Christmas time Rivière officially returned to Catholicism.

1914–1918   Publication of sections of Rivière's Rimbaud study in the *NRF*. When the war broke out, Rivière was called up as a sergeant in the 220th Infantry Regiment. He was captured on 24 August 1914 and spent nearly three years as a prisoner of war in Germany. Isolated from family and friends, Rivière withdrew into himself and struggled for spiritual perfection; he traced the course of his progress in fourteen private notebooks published in 1974, under the title *Carnets*. Classified as physically unfit for further active duty, Rivière spent from June 1917 to early the following summer in Switzerland. He spent the year giving lectures and preparing himself to assume leadership of the *NRF* once the war was over.

1919   As director of the *NRF,* Rivière guided the review through the chaotic postwar era. He gained the respect and admiration of everyone with whom he came into contact for his intellectual rigor and his fairness on all issues.

1920   11 March, birth of Rivière's son Alain, named for his brother-in-law who disappeared during a battle in the early days of World War I, in September 1914.

1922   Publication of The novel *Aimée*.

1923   Lecture series on Proust and Freud at the Vieux-
        Colombier theater in Paris (repeated in March 1924
        in Geneva and Lausanne).

1924   In December: debate with Ramon Fernandez on
        moralism and literature in Geneva and Lausanne.

1925   14 February, Rivière's unexpected death in Paris
        of typhoid fever.

Chapter One

A Sketch of Rivière's Life: From the Calm of Bordeaux to the Cultural Activity of Paris

Childhood and Adolescence in Bordeaux

Before we begin to examine in detail the course of Rivière's psychological and literary evolution, we must first outline the nature of his cultural background, briefly discuss certain significant biographical details, and summarize certain of the literary attitudes in vogue in the late nineteenth century. In doing so we shall be able to situate Rivière's experience with respect to his times and understand more clearly the framework of his personal and his specifically literary development.

Jacques Rivière was born on 15 July 1886 in the southwestern French port city of Bordeaux on the Garonne River, where the summer heat and oppressively calm air were often so overwhelming as to force its inhabitants into a state of almost complete immobility. If any wind at all blew in from the sea or up from the sandy plains to the south, the breeze only served to intensify the feeling of lethargy. The area south of Bordeaux, which was called *les landes,* stretched as far down the coast as Biarritz and was, until the nineteenth century, one of the most desolate sections of France. Originally an unproductive region of barren flatlands, shifting dunes, and billowing sea grass, *les landes* were transformed into vast, carefully cultivated maritime pine forests in the late eighteenth and nineteenth centuries. An extensive irrigation system was also developed to nourish the trees and to guard against the danger of brush fires, which were a constant threat during the dry season. In Rivière's time the area, although economically important, was very lonely and sparsely inhabited, and its proximity to Bordeaux contributed to the sense of paralyzing stillness which Rivière felt enveloped the city.

Rivière was the son of a distinguished physician who was professor of obstetrics at the University of Bordeaux and later became head of the maternity section at the university hospital, and he was the eldest of four children (Jacques, Pierre, Jeanne, and Marc). While Jacques was growing up, the family lived in the second floor apartment of a seventeenth-century house, 12 rue Devise, in the old section of the city near the river. He would often sit for hours at one of the apartment's windows, captivated by the joys of introspection or dreaming of adventures which would take him far beyond the confines of the city proper.[1] Jacques was shy and very sensitive as a small child, and it is not surprising that he had no rapport whatsoever with his overbearing father, who, from the time of Jacques's early childhood, had mapped out the boy's future career as a professor of Greek and took charge of each step of his education along the way. Because of personality and age differences, Jacques was also somewhat isolated from his brothers and sister and frequently retreated into his private world, where no one could tease him and where he could freely enjoy the scenes his imagination conjured up.

It is important to keep in mind, however, that despite his timidity and introspective tendencies, Jacques was also very active physically. As his critic friend Benjamin Crémieux notes in one of the scores of articles written in honor of Rivière just after his death, "This so-called bookworm adored the physical exhilaration of sports."[2] Jacques eagerly explored both the city of Bordeaux itself and the surrounding area on foot, on a bicycle, or in a train, inspecting the contours of the land and marveling at its varied structural configurations in much the same way that he would one day analyze literary works. As a young man he was also fascinated by the then newly invented automobile and the airplane and rejoiced at the possibilities which they opened up in the realm of travel and adventure. The enthusiasm and dedication with which he engaged in physical activity also inspired his earliest intellectual undertakings. While Jacques was still only a very young teenager, for example, he wrote and directed a melodramatic play for his brothers and sister entitled *Les Noces sanglantes*, and in 1901 and 1902 he and his brother Marc put together a literary newsletter entitled *L'Avenir*.[3] Already Jacques's personal interests were quite far removed from those which his father intended for him to pursue, and their relationship became increasingly more tense and strained.

The only person in his immediate family to whom Jacques felt very close in his childhood was his mother, Reine Fernaud Rivière. Guided by her own sensitivity, she understood his needs and gave him the affection and encouragement his father was unable to offer. Like her own mother, Madame Rivière was an ardent, orthodox, but unpretentious Catholic, and Jacques's initial experience with religion was greatly influenced by the simple sincerity of her faith. Unfortunately, Jacques's mother died in 1896 when he was ten years old; with the disappearance of the person whom he loved and respected the most, the young boy felt totally abandoned. His father, preoccupied with his own career and plans for Jacques's academic future, had no real interest in his eldest son's personal problems, and neither the presence of his brothers and sister nor the concern of his maternal aunts could lessen his increasing sense of loneliness and anxiety. When Jacques's father remarried in 1901, the feeling of isolation and rejection became even more acute. In her desire to start a new life with Jacques's father, the boy's stepmother insisted that the family move and sold nearly everything in the old apartment. Jacques was now not only desolate but completely uprooted. The only remaining point of stability in his life was his grandmother's home at Cenon, a little to the southwest of Bordeaux, where he had experienced his happiest moments as a young child and where he spent increasingly more time since his mother's death. But because of his father's growing social obligations and his desire that Jacques participate in them, even this haven was often denied him. The only course of action open to Jacques at this time was

to excel in his studies at the Lycée in Bordeaux and wait patiently
until the time when he could leave to study in Paris.

A little later in life Rivière concretized some of his most vivid
memories from his early years in Bordeaux in a group of four
lyrical meditations which express the ambivalence of his relationship to his past. In "Méditation sur l'Extrême-Occident,"
"Le Chemin de fer," "Les Beaux Jours," and "Histoire de Noé
Sarambuca," all of which were written between 1907 and 1911,
Rivière presents a poeticized version of some of his most striking
childhood impressions. In each of these works his emotional attachment to the Bordeaux area and his interest in topography,
or the exploration of the intricacies of the earth's surface structure,
are the point of departure for lyrical commentaries which go far
beyond the limits of simple descriptive texts.

In "Méditation sur l'Extrême-Occident," for example, the most
confused of the four short pieces and the first to appear in print,
Rivière philosophizes on the secret symbolism of specific geographical areas and the effects of this symbolism on the individuals
who live there. He tries to define the philosophical significance
of the section of France that he knows the best and which has
left its mark on him, but he gets so carried away by the rhythm
of his own rhetoric that he ends up leaving the reader in a state
of perplexed frustration. He discourses at length on what he feels
are the metaphysical connotations of the coastal region near Bordeaux, which seems to bow respectfully before the mysterious
immensity of the sea just as "the soul of the West bows down
before the Unknowable."[4] At this point in his discussion Rivière
begins to describe the philosophical differences between the Christian Western world, which confidently accepts religious myster-
ies, and the non-Christian Orient, which deliberately equates the
incomprehensible with nothingness and refuses to acknowledge
the existence of anything it cannot fully understand. From there
he goes on to praise what he terms the three special forces or
virtues of the West—its metaphysics, its religion, and most of
all its music. This last, a manifestation of the creative imagination, constitutes in Rivière's eyes "the prolongation of metaphysics into the unknowable, a direct attempt to enter into

mystery."[5] Music, he concludes, compensates for the insufficiencies of reason and enables man to accept emotionally what he cannot understand intellectually.

In the second of his childhood-inspired works to be published entitled "Le Chemin de fer," Rivière leaves the confused realm of private spiritual symbolism. He turns his attention to a much more down-to-earth subject and reflects on the particular value for an individual of a journey by train. Since one passes through a number of different landscapes in a train, this mode of transportation enables the traveler to grasp first hand both the variety and the continuity of the earth's surface. This kind of journey allows one to combine intense pleasure with understanding because, as Rivière emphasizes, "Movement is the instrument of knowledge"[6] and makes it possible for the traveler to comprehend the details of a particular terrain in relation to the geographical structure of the region as a whole.

Rivière's third and most directly autobiographical description of childhood memories was published in the *NRF* in 1910. Its title, "Les Beaux Jours," came from a painting which Fournier admired in a Paris exhibit and described in a letter to Rivière. In this short, impressionistic piece he meditates on life in Bordeaux during sultry summer days. Rivière emphasizes the intolerable calm of this "sluggish Atlantic city,"[7] where even the screeching blasts of sirens and train whistles fade almost immediately in the stagnant air. He relives, rather than recalls, the feeling of inexplicable despair that haunted him after the loss of his mother and still persists in the present. As Rivière acknowledges in the concluding section, "This sweet and deadly country of my childhood—I have carried it with me in my soul."[8] The atmosphere of calm and poignant sadness which he associates with Bordeaux is an integral part of his personality, and he must struggle arduously in young adulthood to shake off the psychological lassitude it inspires.

Although descriptions of Bordeaux and its ambivalent influence often dominated Rivière's childhood imaginings, he would at times leave the city and its melancholy inertia far behind. In "Histoire de Noé Sarambuca," the last of his childhood-centered

pieces to be published and the most creative, Rivière's dreams
carry him and the imaginary character whose actions he describes
to mysterious, unknown realms. Like the orphaned child Noé
Sarambuca, who was animated by "a great thirst for knowledge"[9]
and explored the labyrinthine corridors of his aunts' old house
in order to learn as much as he could about his immediate surroundings, Rivière, too, strove to understand the complexities
of the exterior world, struggled to be initiated into "the knowledge of things."[10] Alone in his hidden, deserted tower, Noé
dreamed at night of traveling over the sea to the four corners of
the earth guided by an instinctive tactile sense of orientation. In
a similar fashion, Rivière longed for adventure and contact with
distant unknowns to fulfill his own desire for concrete knowledge.
He sometimes managed to shake off the monotonous restraints
of routine existence and take flight into rich, vibrant fantasies
of continuous motion where "Like a soothsayer . . . he saw."[11]
Through his reveries, Rivière, like Noé, caught fleeting glimpses
of another, more authentic kind of reality and began to understand
"the force of things around him."[12]

     The restless, disorienting visions Rivière conjured up in "His-
toire de Noé Sarambuca" and his other childhood-inspired pieces
reveal the fertility of his imagination and suggest the affirmative
role of dream activity in the development of the human psyche.
They indicate the importance of imaginary adventure in his life
and also bring into full view Rivière's equally strong desire to
learn as much as possible about the real world around him.
Through railroad journeys and hikes in the woodlands of his
native province, he tried to touch the many-textured surface of
the earth and understand how its diverse elements interacted to
form a whole. The power of his imagination, coupled with this
need to experience close, physical contact with reality and see
things accurately, struggled against his lassitude. These equally
strong opposing tendencies kept him from losing all sense of
perspective and giving in completely to self-pity.

     It is important to remember that Rivière wrote the works
dealing with his childhood several years after he had left Bordeaux
and over a particularly crucial four-year period in his evolution.

Although they express, to a great extent, his impressions of the region and his reactions to it, his vision is nonetheless greatly influenced by the experiences he had undergone since his departure from Bordeaux, by his own changing philosophical attitudes, and by those of authors whose works he was reading at the time he was writing these meditations.

Prewar Experience in Paris

In the autumn of 1903 an anxious but eager Rivière left Bordeaux to continue his studies at the prestigious Lycée Lakanal in Paris, where the students worked diligently to prepare for the highly competitive entrance exams into the Ecole Normale Supérieure, the most rigorous of France's institutions of higher education, which prepared the country's most distinguished university professors and scholars. During the early months of his stay in Paris at the Lycée, Rivière gradually became friends with Henri Fournier.[13] Despite their vast personality differences (Fournier was as rowdy and mischievous as Rivière was quiet and serious), the two young men were drawn together by their passion for Symbolist poetry and their exhilaration at being in Paris. Their friendship developed quite rapidly from the time they listened to their instructor recite from the anthology *Tel qu'en songe* by the late-nineteenth-century poet Henri de Régnier just before the Christmas recess. Glancing at one another during the recitation, Rivière and Fournier realized that they were in a very profound sense kindred spirits, and their friendship continued to grow until Fournier's death in the early days of World War I.

Both Rivière and Fournier were at this time in their development under the spell of the Symbolist poets. Although the importance of the Symbolists was beginning to wane during the years that Rivière and Fournier were at the Lycée Lakanal, these poets nevertheless continued to influence French poetry and literary attitudes in general during the entire first decade of the twentieth century. The interest in poetry as a symbol-making activity developed gradually during the second half of the nineteenth century in France; it reached its culminating point in the

efforts of the elitist Symbolist school which almost exclusively
dominated French poetry from approximately 1885 to 1900, and
whose effects lingered for years after.

The poets who so captured the attention of Rivière and Fournier
were mainly those minor poets such as Henri de Régnier, Jules
Laforgue, Maurice Maeterlinck, and Villiers de l'Isle-Adam who
were directly associated with the Symbolist school. Later on they
would read the works of the more important poets associated with
the development of Symbolism, such as Baudelaire, Verlaine, and
Mallarmé, but at this early point in their evolution, it was the
creatively limited works of the minor Symbolists which so attracted their attention. Both Rivière and Fournier were drawn
as if by a magnetic force to the ethereal quality of this poetry,
which left the mundane concerns of the everyday world far behind.
The act of reading these poets enabled them to indulge in self-
centered fantasies, and, at the same time, it sanctioned this activity under the emblem of poetic introspection.

In addition to the enormous influence of the Symbolists on the
young, psychologically vulnerable Rivière was that of the late-
nineteenth and early-twentieth-century novelist from the province
of Lorraine, Maurice Barrès. As indicated by the title of his early
trilogy *Culte du Moi,* Barrès was an ardent individualist who
emphasized the uniqueness of the human psyche and delighted
in self-analysis. Later on in his career he changed his point of
emphasis, stressing the link between the individual and his native
region, a change of direction which in turn led him to become
a passionate French nationalist. Rivière was influenced mainly
by the egocentric qualities of Barrès's works, which reinforced
certain attitudes of the Symbolists and nourished his own tendencies toward psychological self-indulgence.

In the summer of 1905, Rivière failed the entrance exams to
the prestigious Ecole Normale, but he did receive a scholarship
to prepare his *licence* (the general equivalent of an American Master
of Arts degree) that fall at the University of Bordeaux. He spent
that year working toward his degree, and the following autumn,
in September 1906, he began his year of compulsory military
service garrisoned near Bordeaux. As his letters to Fournier, who

was still in Paris, clearly reveal, Rivière detested the mindless regimentation of military life and the vulgarity of his fellow soldiers. But he likewise reveled in the intensity of the physical activity, which brought him to the edge and sometimes beyond what he thought was the limit of his endurance. Rivière also had enough free time during this year to continue his academic pursuits and completed his *licence* in the summer of 1907.

During the same year Rivière also became acquainted with Fournier's younger sister Isabelle, who had moved to Paris and was living with her brother. Their affection for one another grew rapidly despite the fact that they saw each other only briefly during vacation periods, and on 24 August 1909 they were married. Isabelle had a profound stabilizing and calming effect on Rivière's hypersensitive nervous system. She provided both the emotional security and the intellectual companionship he so greatly needed to develop to the fullest of his potential. Isabelle helped Rivière to turn his gaze outward toward others, to enjoy more fully the small wonders of everyday life, and eventually to understand the importance of religion in relation to his literary interests. More than anyone else or any other outside influence, it was Isabelle and her quiet encouragement which helped Rivière resolve his spiritual dilemma.

Although Rivière ceased to practice Catholicism during his years at the Lycée Lakanal, and attempted to seek answers elsewhere, he was always haunted by the shadow of Christianity. Indeed it was his desire to solve his religious difficulties which prompted him in January 1907 to write to the distinguished Catholic dramatist, poet, and essayist Paul Claudel, who at that time was with the French diplomatic service in China. Claudel was eager to help Rivière in any way that he could, but the young man systematically rejected each course of action Claudel urged him to follow. For several years Rivière argued with Claudel and struggled against the force of his influence, which in some ways resembled the overbearing strength of his father. At this point in his experience, Rivière felt that his attitudes were much closer to the concepts of self-development and personal sincerity which were expressed in the works of André Gide than they were to the well-defined certitude which Claudel represented.

He drew away from Claudel and became friends on both a personal and professional level with Gide, who stressed the importance of mapping out one's own path in life. Gide did not try to force Rivière to accept any one point of view over another and provided the kind of unrestricted encouragement which Rivière needed at this time in his life. In 1909, the *Nouvelle Revue Française,* the review which Gide had worked at organizing for many years, began to appear monthly; Rivière was immediately welcomed as a regular contributor and was thus launched in the career of his choice. While he pursued his literary activities with the *NRF,* however, Rivière continued to agonize about spiritual issues. By 1913 he finally managed to work out the most serious of his philosophical difficulties and, inspired by the recently renewed fervor of his wife, Isabelle, he officially returned to Catholicism at Christmas time that year.[14]

The War Years and Their Aftermath

When the war broke out the following August, Rivière was called into service and sent almost immediately into battle. After only a few days at the front, however, he was captured by the Germans and spent nearly the next three years in a prisoner-of-war camp. During his captivity, Rivière underwent an intense spiritual renewal, and his faith far surpassed the level of his commitment at the time of his formal return to the Church in 1913. As we shall see when we examine Rivière's war journal, his faith reached mystical heights during the years of his separation from family and friends. Religion was Rivière's principal source of stability in a totally alien situation and one of the few manifestations of continuity with his past which could be maintained during the period of his captivity.

After the war was over, a physically weakened but intellectually eager Rivière took over the arduous directorship of the *NRF.* From this time onward, religion no longer played an active role in his public life, but his commitment to justice, his deep concern for his fellow human beings, and his open—mindedness on literary, social, and political issues attest to the truly Christian nature of his attitudes. Rivière led the *NRF* through what was without question one of the stormiest, most chaotic periods of change when many contradictory voices were all clamoring, not only to be heard, but to dominate the literary, intellectual, and social scene. When others of his generation were reacting indignantly to the anarchic tactics of the Dadaists and later the Surrealists, Rivière expressed his gratitude to them for having dared to shake the foundations of language and attack the very concept of literature itself. Although he opposed many of their attitudes, he nevertheless recognized the necessity for asking the radical questions which they posed. In the early 1920s, Rivière also began to study the then revolutionary theories of Sigmund Freud, and he championed the cause of Marcel Proust, personally overseeing the publication of Proust's epic literary undertaking *A la Recherche du temps perdu.*

Rivière's intellectual adaptability and critical flexibility met their severest test when he received the confused, tortured poems of the young, totally unknown Antonin Artaud. Rivière refused to publish Artaud's poems because of their overall incoherence. But the very fact that Rivière corresponded with Artaud and asked the younger man's permission to publish the correspondence exchanged between them clearly indicates the profound effect which Artaud had on him. It also reveals the extent of Rivière's effort to understand the kind of enigmatic problem tormenting Artaud in relation to the crisis concerning the very definition of the term literature which was dominating the Paris literary scene at the time. As their correspondence reveals, Rivière eventually recognized the unique and totally private nature of Artaud's dilemma and understood that it had nothing to do with the specifically literary problems which other writers had to confront. Nevertheless, despite the intensity of Artaud's suffering, Rivière pleaded with him to continue struggling against it and to continue trying to seize his thoughts, even if they were only fragments, for the only alternative was complete mental disintegration and death.

Ironically, Rivière, who stressed again and again his own commitment to life in his letters to Artaud, had himself only a short time to live. In the winter of 1925 he contracted typhoid fever and, after one last heroic struggle, died on 14 February. But although Rivière died very young, his passionate dedication to truth, understanding, and open-mindedness live on in his personal and critical writings and in the tradition of the *NRF* itself to inspire future generations to develop themselves to the fullest as he had done in his own life.

Chapter Two

From Dreams to Reality: Rivière's Early Development and Experience with Claudel

The Revelations of Rivière's Early Letters to Fournier

The nine-year exchange of letters between Jacques Rivière and Alain-Fournier is one of the most revealing and informative literary chronicles of early—twentieth-century France. Unlike the vast published correspondence cycles of more important, more well known authors such as Paul Claudel or André Gide, which begin when they are fairly mature adults, the letters exchanged between Rivière and Fournier trace their development as two of the period's most representative figures from late adolescence to adulthood. Through their totally uninhibited correspondence we can follow the rhythm of their intellectual and emotional maturation on nearly a day-to-day basis. We can likewise witness almost firsthand the gradual emerging of the aesthetic and philosophical changes that would eventually bring about a complete reexamination of cultural attitudes. Along with openly expressing the most intimate causes of their personal joys and anguish in their letters, Rivière and Fournier also enjoyed sparring with one another, playing intellectual games, and, at times, discoursing with ironic glee on some minute literary point. With the strength of their friendship as a pivotal point, each one of the correspondents could be completely honest, knowing that the other would understand the strength of the personal commitment which inspired even the most critical remarks. Since neither feared alienating the other, the young men could speak with often brutal frankness. There is no sham, no pretense in their rapport. And it is this openness, coupled with their reciprocal insight into their private dilemmas, that makes their correspondence so valuable in relation both to their creative and critical works and to their literary era.

The letters exchanged between Rivière and Fournier provided each of the young men with a framework in which to examine his individual reactions to literary and philosophical issues and to test out his ideas on the other. The correspondence begins with two letters which Rivière wrote in January 1905, when he was in the school infirmary and could not have visitors. But it was not until the following summer that they started to correspond on a regular basis. At this time Fournier decided to spend a few months in London improving his English. Rivière, who had failed to pass the Ecole Normale entrance exams, returned to Bordeaux to rest and begin preparing his *licence* there in the fall. From this summer on, the two friends would never again spend any considerable amount of time together. External events over which they had no control and individual career commitments kept them apart, and they saw each other only for brief vacation periods. Consequently their correspondence provided their only source of day-to-day contact; it was the only way they could communicate with one another and nourish the bond between them.

The opening paragraphs of Rivière's very first letter, from January 1905, provide the initial key to one of his lifelong preoccupations. "Our first duty is to keep from acting literary in our lives. . . . Let us try to remain simple and sincere toward ourselves. . . . By following one's safe little line of interior truth, one is sure not to deceive oneself."[1] Even at this uncertain point in his life when he was still an adolescent schoolboy, we can already detect Rivière's disgust with professional authors and critics who play hypocritical roles and betray the integrity of their convictions in order to assure themselves of a public following. We can also discern his early commitment to the concept of personal sincerity, which would become even more important later on in his evolution. These youthful remarks clearly suggest the general direction Rivière would follow in his own effort to discover the specific areas of his potential and take full advantage of his possibilities.

Rivière's next letters, written in the summer of 1905, deal mainly with his recent academic defeat and his intention to concentrate on music and philosophy at the university in Bordeaux in the hopes of eventually being able to develop a philosophy of music theory. But, at the same time, they also begin to outline his personal literary convictions. One of his most far-reaching statements is his negative reaction to the sterile artificiality of the novel as it then existed, coupled with the first general indications as to what he felt the genre could and should be. "Very frank avowal: I don't like the novel. . . . There is another way to escape from the artifice of the novel. . . . It is to create a novel which would be an absolute, complete world, independent of everything. . . . The poet echoes what he hears in himself and expresses it. The true novelist invents and discovers something" (*Corr. R-F,* 1:46–47). Through these remarks Rivière indirectly outlines the struggle between subjectivity and objectivity which would soon become so crucial an issue in his own maturation process. He also briefly touches upon the opposition he sees developing between subjective creation and invention and introduces his concept of the novel as an art form which must be totally free from all external pressures. As we shall see, these are some of the same principles he would draw upon, for example, when organizing his pivotal essay "Le Roman d'aventure" nearly eight years later and, to an even greater degree, when writing his revolutionary postwar lectures on Proust. The preoccupations sketched here would remain constant throughout his life and inspire some of his most perceptive critical works.

During these same early months of their separation, Rivière also describes in detail his recurrent attacks of depression and hypersensitivity and specifies for Fournier the nature of his fascination for the exoticism of Maurice Barrès—one of the authors to play a decisive role in his personality development and the first to figure heavily in his correspondence. In his initial comments

on Barrès, Rivière emphasizes his natural disposition to accept
and exult in Barrès's provocative cultivation of the ego at a time
when he himself is floundering at how to define himself, and he
also indicates how clearly he understands the terms and the limits
of Barrès's aesthetic. In subsequent letters, Rivière goes on to
describe his reaction to specific technical aspects of Barrès's novels
and again stresses that "all the Dandyism, the Ecstasy, the Swoon-
ing—I experienced them before learning the name Barrès, and
I live them at every moment . . ." (*Corr. R-F,* 1:105). In other
words, Barrès's hypersensitive subjectivism corresponded to Rivière's own psychological state at the time. The attitudes expressed in Barrès's novels only reflect what Rivière had already
been experiencing. He yielded to the seductive charm of novels
such as *Le Jardin de Bérénice* or *Les Déracinés* because Barrès's
situation so closely resembled his own to begin with and because
they provided an ultrarefined context for self-examination. Alone
in Bordeaux in the summer and fall of 1905, Rivière reveled in
Barrèsian ego analysis, feeding masochistically on both his melancholy and his boredom. The self-conscious and self-induced
isolation he felt as a child after his mother's death assumed even
more overwhelming proportions during this sensitive time of late
adolescence. It temporarily dominated his vision and blocked out
other outside stimuli.

During the same period that Rivière was reading Barrès and
living the attitudes expressed in his works, he was also dabbling
in philosophical studies, concentrating on Plato, Schopenhauer,
and Hegel. He likewise continued to devour the works of the
minor Symbolists. The experience of reading these poets, coupled
with the influence of Barrès and the attraction of Platonic ide-
alism, heightened his tendency to retreat behind a screen of
introspection. Rivière and Fournier, as well as countless others
who were born in the last two decades of the nineteenth century,
could be considered case studies revealing the effect of Symbolism's charm on adolescent sensibilities. It was, as we have seen,
the ethereal reverberations of Symbolist poetry that had first
brought Rivière and Fournier together at the Lycée Lakanal and
made them realize how much they had in common. As Rivière

notes in his introduction to Fournier's anthology of short stories and poems entitled *Miracles,* "I don't know if it is possible to make people understand what Symbolism was for those who *lived* it. A spiritual atmosphere, a comforting place of exile, or rather of repatriation, a paradise."[2] It was impossible for them to resist the spell triggered by their contact with Régnier's "Great winds come from across the sea."[3]

One of the most lucid and most accurate statements concerning Symbolism's method and intent comes, curiously enough, from Rivière himself. In the introductory section to his article entitled "Le Roman d'aventure," which outlines Rivière's plan for general aesthetic reform, he summarizes the main points of the Symbolist attitude and analyzes the consequences of its influence. Stemming from an extreme self-consciousness and the desire to concretize an emotional reaction to a particular stimulus through subtly suggestive images, the Symbolists' works revealed a totally subjective attitude which scorned contact with common, everyday reality. As an aesthetic movement Symbolism offered an elitist form of refuge to those who had convinced themselves that they were too sensitive to confront everyday life. Moreover, Rivière stresses in his commentary that "The Symbolists knew only the pleasures of weary people . . . they lived in a twilight atmosphere. . . . The world had worn itself out, it had gradually assumed a kind of weakness and ideality" (*NE,* 246). It was much easier to deny the importance of reality than to deal with it, therefore the Symbolists constructed elaborate and frequently incomprehensible verbal structures to justify their inertia.

Both fascinated and encouraged by this ultrarefined attitude, Rivière was in no hurry to change. He thoroughly enjoyed indulging in long, drawn out passages of self-analysis, emphasizing, for example, that "True reality for me is general. . . . I formulate general ideas while endowing them with a certain color, a certain precise beauty" (*Corr. R-F,* 1:131). In other words, despite his desire "to classify, to put in order" (*Corr. R-F,* 1:131), he, at this point, thought sensually and automatically endowed theoretical generalities with specific, easily perceivable qualities. As already indicated by his childhood struggle between the real and imaginary and by his comments on inertia and motion made in slightly earlier letters to Fournier, many different opposing tendencies coexisted within him and were struggling for ascendency. There was as yet no definite distinction between the abstract and the concrete, no order in his thought process.

Further on in this same confusing but particularly revealing letter, Rivière turned to another related topic of self-interest, discoursing at length on the intense pleasure he derived from fragmented desires that lead nowhere. He became so involved in the psychological intricacies and "the voluptuousness of this destructive analysis" (*Corr. R-F,* 1:134) that he appeared to lose control and fall victim to the force of his own rhetoric. But at the very moment when he seemed to whirl about most dizzily, he stopped short and cautioned Fournier, "Don't take me seriously" (*Corr. R-F,* 1:135). He openly acknowledged the exaggerated, artificial quality of his comments, making sure that his friend caught the ironic undertone and revealing his own degree of self-awareness. He never lost himself completely in his intellectual and emotional meanderings. As indicated by his remarks in this letter, he maintained a certain degree of detachment which kept him from viewing his problems too tragically and made it possible for him to consider his individual situation in a larger, more down-to-earth framework.

Rivière's Encounter with Claudel's Literary Creations

In his very next letter to his confidant, Rivière again referred to his fragmented desires but this time in a context which quickly opened up startling new dimensions in his effort to define himself. His contact with another author, Paul Claudel, briefly mentioned for the first time in a slightly earlier letter dated 5 November 1905, made him realize almost immediately how far he had already progressed in relation to the narrow developmental framework of both Barrès and the Symbolists.[4] His comments, based on a quick reading of the poetry of *Les Muses* and on the first part of Claudel's play *Tête d'Or* were at first hesitant and somewhat ambivalent.[5] But after finishing all five of the plays in the anthology *L'Arbre,* Rivière recognized the immensity of Claudel's inspiration and cried out enthusiastically that "He is greater than Dante. . . . Never perhaps has one cast a more essential glance on the things of this life. . . . We have a philosopher dramatist" (*Corr. R-F,* 1:179). As he continued to experience the disorienting influence of Claudel's early works, Rivière's enthusiasm for the author and for the realities of this earth developed proportionately. It was as if his childhood tendency to retreat from society and the lure of Symbolist escapism, both of which had somewhat dominated his personality up to this time, began noticeably to disintegrate when confronted by the marvelous complexities of the real world which Claudel described in his dramas.

During the next several months, references to Claudel's works and to their transforming effect played a more and more important role in Rivière's letters. He indicated how overwhelmed he was, on the one hand, by "this bottomless anguish of Cébès, by the 'Nothing exists' of Besme, by the appalling anxiety of Tête d'Or,"[6] and, on the other, by the rich, sensual quality of Claudel's inspiration as revealed in *L'Arbre.* Rivière's attention was at first focused on the natural or essentially earthly significance of Claudel's attitudes as expressed through the very title of his dramatic anthology. The tree, though remaining deeply rooted in the ground, pushes upward to reach the light of the sun. Rivière stressed that, like the tree which grows in union with the rhythms of the earth's seasonal changes, man, too, must develop his natural tendencies as completely as possible. As he had stated in his very first letter to Fournier, every person must follow his own "internal truth" (*Corr. R-F,* 1:9). Only in this way can an individual even begin to attain spiritual fulfillment, for "God is the primitive direction preserved to the end, the bounding movement of the tree which nothing has thwarted, which rests in its fulfillment" (*Corr. R-F,* 1:180).

In this context the actions of the elder sister Mara in *La Jeune Fille Violaine,* who remains attached to the earth, take on over-whelmingly positive connotations. And the detachment of Violaine, who turns away from her love for Jacques Hury and strives for supernatural heroism, becomes sinful. By rejecting earthly relationships and succumbing to the temptation of self-sacrifice, Violaine ends up betraying her human identity (*Corr. R-F,* 1:221–23). In trying to be more than human, she severs all ties with her surroundings and loses the possibility of attaining an authentic, integrated kind of spiritual fulfillment.

During the spring and summer of 1906, however, Rivière continued to read and reread Claudel's plays and the prose poems of *Connaissance de l'Est* in the light of certain of his theoretical essays such as *Connaissance du Temps*. As he did so, his exuberance and the focus of his attention changed direction somewhat. He ceased to emphasize the all-important necessity of developing one's strictly human capabilities and became more and more convinced that the uniqueness of Claudel's inspiration resided in the harmony he revealed among the various elements of the physical world and then between the temporal and the spiritual realms. Rivière's intent is quite clear when he describes "the impression of profound unity, of penetration of the soul and nature, of confusion and of intimate communion between the physical being and the spirit" (*Corr. R-F,* 1:300) and when he rejoices at how this corresponds to his own expanding vision, "It is so beautiful, so completely harmonious, so close to my heart" (*Corr. R-F,* 1:300).

As Rivière's understanding of Claudel's world-view grew more and more complete over the summer, he also modified his attitude concerning the relationship between the characters Mara and Violaine. Though he still felt drawn to Mara's passionate energy and to her dynamic attachment to Jacques and her heritage, he also acknowledged the sublime dignity of Violaine's offering as she gave up everything in order to ascend to God and fulfilled her human destiny in the process. He finally recognized the singular importance of Violaine's action in relation both to her sister and to Claudel's earlier protagonists; he understood why man should not remain so passionately attached to the earth and to the past as Mara was, refusing to relinquish her possessions for an intangible goal.

In November 1906 Fournier wrote to tell Rivière of a recent discovery he had made concerning Claudel: "He is a Catholic"

(*Corr. R-F,* 1:380). Soon after receiving this news, Rivière learned from the recently converted Bordeaux man of letters Gabriel Frizeau that Claudel had strong missionary tendencies and was inspired by the desire to bring lost souls back to the Church. Rivière was both surprised and profoundly shaken by this information. He was anxious because of his own spiritual restlessness and also because of the violent, somewhat unorthodox quality of Claudel's attitudes as expressed in the plays collected in *L'Arbre.*[7] He was so struck by Frizeau's comments about Claudel's messianic aspirations that he wrote to Fournier, "He has almost completely modified my conception, I see him now as a Christian . . ." (*Corr. R-F,* 1:423).

It must be noted, however, that although Rivière's image of Claudel the man changed radically, his overall conception of Claudel's literary vision remained substantially intact. As clearly indicated in his letters to Fournier, Rivière had worked out the initial version of an article on Claudel in the summer and fall of 1906, and completed it only four days after the letter describing his conversation with Frizeau. On 26 December 1906 he wrote to Fournier stressing that "I finished my article this evening, that is to say, I can now spend my time revising it. It is done in general" (*Corr. R-F,* 1:430). And the interpretation of Claudel's work developed in the final version of the article, which appeared in the review *L'Occident* in the autumn of 1907 and was later included in *Etudes,* is essentially the same. Although it is entitled "Paul Claudel, Poète chrétien," it reaffirms and amplifies the same ideas described in his letters to Fournier the previous year, before he knew anything at all concerning Claudel's ties with Catholicism.

During much of the year 1907, Rivière agonized over his article on Claudel and his own spiritual dilemma. He rethought his whole approach and reflected on the accuracy of his interpretations. Confronted by the overwhelming force of Claudel's missionary zeal, he wondered if he would ever have the audacity to reexamine the problem of Claudel's inspiration, much less publish a completed study. But with Fournier's encouragement and helpful critical comments, he persevered in his task. What is partic-

ularly important about Rivière's work on Claudel during this
period is that, in the end, he decided to return almost word for
word to the original draft. As he admitted to Fournier in August
1907, "After great struggles I returned almost literally to the
first version" (*Corr. R-F,* 2:147). After months of rethinking and
rewriting, Rivière felt that his comments in the original version
were the most accurate and the most faithful to the textual intricacies of the works themselves. Though he enlarged upon and
greatly deepened his appreciation as he read each of Claudel's new
works, and would continue to do so, he had already grasped the
nucleus of Claudel's thought and the continuity of his dramatic
vision. Consequently his basic orientation did not change
substantially.

The only aspect of the analysis which continued to trouble
Rivière and where he feared that he had perhaps gone too far
afield (as he indicated indirectly to Fournier and openly in a letter
to Frizeau) was his continued insistence that "The only crime
according to him [Claudel] was the exchange of, the renunciation
of one's role, the abandoning of the struggle."[8] Rivière was ap-
prehensive about Claudel's reaction to this aspect of his study
because he did not wish to alienate Claudel or impose his own
ideas on Claudel's works. However, he need not have feared the
older man's wrath. When Claudel received the first two parts of
the *Occident* article, he wrote enthusiastically to Rivière in January
1908, "This is the first time that a methodical study has been
done on my work, and, even for the author, it is quite informative
to see oneself objectified and examined by a pair of attentive
eyes."[9]

As far as the specific ideas about which Rivière was so appre-
hensive are concerned, Claudel himself dismissed them as simple
exaggerations. He was delighted and impressed with the subtlety
of Rivière's insight, and when he received the concluding section
of Rivière's analysis, Claudel once again exclaimed, "I am very
proud and very happy about your study. How many things you
have gotten out of what seemed to many people (perhaps even
to myself) to be an inextricable jumble."[10]

Rivière's article on Claudel constitutes his first substantial effort at literary criticism. It reveals the freshness of his vision, the sensitivity of his perceptions, and the exuberance of his response to Claudel. Quite understandably, it also reveals the hesitancy of his approach and his lack of experience as a critic. Until the fall of 1907, the only things Rivière had published were several short reviews of artistic events taking place in Paris, and "Méditation sur l'Extrême-Occident," his confused, highly personal reflections on the spiritual symbolism of the Bordeaux countryside, which appeared in *L'Occident* only three months before his Claudel article came out. Rivière's complex three-part study of Claudel's inspiration emphasizes above all else the plentitude of Claudel's universe. For Claudel, "The world is a totality, an infinitely complex harmony where all things invoke and complement one another. . . . An equilibrium is established, a general correspondence is developed; the world is balanced in an ineffable unity . . ." (*E, 67*).

After elaborating on the specific nature of this harmony in the first part of his analysis, Rivière turns his attention in the second section to the effects of original sin, and he examines in detail in Claudel's works the role of man, whose task it is to administer the earth and "unceasingly represent Creation to the Creator" (*E, 79*). Finally, in the third part of his analysis, Rivière concentrates on man's reintegration with God through the sacrifice of a Violaine, who "experiences an awesome, a delicious, and secret blooming in her heart" (*E, 90*). He greatly expands his earlier comments made in letters to Fournier throughout 1906 concerning the rapport between the natural and the supernatural in Claudel's vision, noting the importance of his apostolic tendencies and using specifically religious terminology. But, at the same time, he continues more than ever to stress the basic sumptuousness of Claudel's imagination and the *two-sided* harmony of his world-view. Though man's ultimate destiny is to worship his Creator, the most efficacious way of approaching God is by entering into direct contact with the things He has created on this earth, by trying to understand the marvelous intricacies of their makeup, and by recognizing that "Each tree has its personality, each little animal its role, each voice its place in the symphony."[11] Like the wide-eyed narrator in Claudel's prose poem "Le Promeneur," man is "The inspector of Creation, the one who verifies the present situation."[12] He would really be derelict in his duty if he closed his eyes and did not savor the splendor around him during the time of his stewardship on the earth.

By living in close contact with Claudel's works from January to early November 1906, when as yet he knew nothing of Claudel's specific religious affiliations, Rivière discovered on his own how the elements of Claudel's dramatic universe functioned, and he understood the essential role of these hesitant early plays in the overall framework of Claudel's career. Much later, in a 1921 article on Claudel's plays, Rivière would again stress the intimate link between man and nature or "the profound union between the creature and creation,"[13] and reaffirm his conception of the cosmic harmony revealed in Claudel's literary universe where "Everything is related,"[14] on both the philosophical and aesthetic levels.

It is also important to note, however, that although Rivière's interpretation of the unity of Claudel's vision remained constant, his personal enthusiasm for Claudel's works began to wane in the years following the publication of his study in *L'Occident*. In 1910, Rivière wrote a brief article entitled "Les Oeuvres lyriques de Claudel," for the *NRF,* in which he concentrates on the stylistic or formal aspects of Claudel's *Odes* and *Hymnes*. The scope of Rivière's interest is now much more limited. He seems to stand further back from the works and to treat Claudel's inspiration with much greater reserve than he had a few years earlier. He singles out, for example, the tumultuous, disordered quality of Claudel's *Odes,* which "rise up from the sensual force of the visions which they transcribe" (*E,* 101) and are carried along by the sheer force of the poet's imagination. They strike out energetically in many different directions from a central emotion, which provides a minimal kind of orientation and draws the reader along in its fluctuating movement. Reading one of Claudel's *Odes* is like "being carried by a . . . ship in the middle of a huge sensual tempest" (*E,* 103). On the other hand, the drama of Claudel's

Hymnes unfolds in a completely different kind of landscape and transcribes the exclusive, solitary, jealously guarded joy of Christian fidelity. In sharp contrast to the seething, somewhat helter-skelter movement of the *Odes,* the stylistic regularity and constant repetition of the *Hymnes* communicate a feeling of "merciless monotony" (*E,* 105) which weighs heavily upon the reader. There is no way to escape from the relentless brilliance of the sun which dominates the *Hymnes.* It sears the land and the human heart, bombarding them with "the cruel light of joy" (*E,* 105), destroying all vestiges of doubt or resistance to its power and suppressing all poetic ambiguity.

Rivière reacts negatively, on the one hand, to the confusion and overall lack of clear intellectual direction in the *Odes* and, on the other, to the oppressive, ever-present sun and fire images in the *Hymnes,* which force the poems into a very restricted framework. There is no margin left for lyrical resonance or spiritual questioning. When Rivière first read Claudel's works, he was overwhelmed by the grandiose, cosmic quality of his inspiration and transcribed the awe he felt for the magnificence and the richness of Claudel's vision into his study for the review *L'Occident.* By 1910, however, Rivière's attitude toward and relationship with Claudel had changed. He had moved beyond the stage of sensitive, enthusiastic comprehension and begun to discern what he saw as some of the limitations of Claudel's creations, which sprang, to a certain extent at least, from the author's complete spiritual certitude. At the same time, as his own evolution as a critic progressed, Rivière began to concentrate more heavily on the formal or specifically aesthetic qualities of Claudel's works, trying to explain the way in which their different elements functioned together to form a satisfying whole. This slowly developing attitude would stand out even more strongly in his postwar article on Claudel where, as he insists in his introduction, "Rather than examine the difficulties which stem from his ideas, I would like to study obstacles of a technical order."[15] In this article Rivière reiterates his admiration for Claudel's early plays and reaffirms his conception of the metaphysical harmony which stands out in all of Claudel's creations and which he had first described in his

Occident study. But in this article Rivière spends most of his time explaining the difficulties that arise from the unusual rhythm of Claudel's poetry (both dramatic and lyric) or from the complicated interweaving of images which develop according to intricate psychological associations.

And in keeping with the evolution of his own aesthetic attitudes, Rivière is now careful to point out the kind of link which he sees between Claudel and the seventeenth-century French Classical writers. For the first time Rivière turns his attention to the specifically aesthetic unity of Claudel's theater explaining the intricate substructure of his plays and describing how each of the elements fits into the author's overall scheme. He emphasizes how this kind of internal harmony sets Claudel apart from the Romantics and "makes Claudel's early plays, in spite of their difficulties, works profoundly related to those of our Classical writers."[16] As we shall see in a later chapter, by as early as 1913 Rivière would come to believe that the greatest possibility for aesthetic renewal lay in trying to integrate the principles of clarity, unity, and internal equilibrium which characterized seventeenth-century French literature with the concerns of the present, thereby creating a new contemporary form of Classicism. And his commitment to this ideal would become even greater after the war when he would take over the running of the *NRF*. Rivière's 1921 article on Claudel stresses, on the one hand, his unchanged conception of Claudel's metaphysical harmony, and, on the other, it clearly reveals the direction Rivière's thought would take in the years ahead.

Rivière's Religious Difficulties and Claudel's Counsel

Although Rivière's vision of Claudel's creative works did not alter in any substantive way when he learned of Claudel's specifically Catholic fervor in late 1906, his attitude toward religion and the possibilities it had to offer him did change dramatically. Raised in a traditional, bourgeois, Catholic environment, Rivière had ceased to practice the ritualistic Catholicism of his childhood at the Lycée Lakanal, when he was on his own living away from

Bordeaux for the first time. In describing Rivière's religious situation, however, we must keep in mind the specific nature and
context of his revolt. Timid but at the same time passionately
curious as a child, Rivière began, at a fairly young age, to question
the simple piety of his maternal grandmother and his great-aunts.
Though he recognized the authenticity of their belief, he could
not share their naive convictions or participate in their enthusiasm. There were too many issues that troubled him even as a
child. He was more and more psychologically isolated from his
immediate family after his mother's death and felt that religion
could offer no real help in his search for truth, understanding,
and self-fulfillment. Somewhat similar to the intellectually stifling atmosphere described in François Mauriac's novels depicting
life in Rivière's native province, religion, at this point in his life,
corresponded to the unhesitating acceptance of involved rituals
and mystifying doctrines. It tolerated no doubts and no questions,
however honest they might be.

It is not at all surprising that, once in Paris, Rivière shunned
all contact with the Catholic Church. Given the nature of his
background and psychological makeup, Rivière could not be as
radical in his rejection of religion as other twentieth-century
French authors would be. The absolute atheism of the later Dadaists, the Surrealists, or certain Existentialists was impossible for
him. His resistance was much more reserved and his rejection
more limited in scope. This comment is not intended, however,
to lessen the overall significance of Rivière's conflict; his anguish
at this time in late adolescence was profoundly authentic and
would continue to plague him intermittently throughout his life.
It merely helps us situate his struggle in relation to the more
overwhelming metaphysical upheaval that would explode during
and after World War I.

Encouraged by Symbolist-inspired escapism and by the appeal
of Barrès's hypersensitive egocentricity, Rivière indulged his introspective tendencies and became convinced of the vanity of
human existence. He tried to define himself in a nonreligious
context, while at the same time never losing all contact with his
past. In the weeks immediately following his discovery of

Claudel's religious affiliation in November 1906, Rivière grew more and more uneasy. While he understood the structure of Claudel's literary vision, he had never come into contact with a *Catholic* who described the world as exuberantly and passionately as Claudel did. Awestruck as he was at the time by the force and the dynamism of Claudel's dramatic universe, he gradually began to view Christianity through Claudel's eyes while simultaneously resisting Claudel's pressure and trying to preserve his independence. Inspired by the way in which "his [Claudel's] genius so marvelously transforms and illuminates" (*Corr. R-F*, 1:410) Catholic doctrine, Rivière started to consider his own situation from another point of view. And in February 1907, he wrote to Claudel for the first time openly seeking his aid in resolving his spiritual dilemma.

The exchange of letters between Rivière and Claudel was triggered by comments which Gabriel Frizeau, the Bordeaux critic and art patron, who was Claudel's first convert, made concerning Claudel's devastating effect on the young poet Alexis Léger (St. John Perse). The correspondence between Rivière and Claudel runs chronologically parallel to the Rivière-Fournier letters written between 1907 and 1914. The majority of the letters dealing with religious issues date from 1907 or 1908, and the correspondence as a whole reveals yet another significant aspect of Rivière's personal development. This time Rivière was not writing to a friend with whom he could be totally open, but to an imposing authority figure whom he wished to impress concerning the depth of his anxiety and the ambivalence of his present attitude toward religion. Part of Rivière earnestly sought calm and certitude, but another equally strong side of his personality thrived on the very anguish he begged Claudel to help him cure.

Although, according to his own admission, he was at times hypocritical in depicting his problem, and although he frequently couched his entreaties in melodramatic terms, Rivière's suffering was nonetheless acute and his plea for help genuinely moving.[17] In his second letter to Claudel (written over a period of ten days), he explains in detail the reasons behind his present turmoil. "Two things will always prevent me from being a Christian: the feeling of the reality of nothingness, [*le néant*] complacency in my despair" (*Corr. R-F,* 2:27). Rivière discovered the concept of *le néant* in Symbolist poems, in Barrès's novels, and, as we shall see in the following chapter, in the writings of André Gide; he also found this attitude expressed in certain sections of Claudel's early works. In Rivière's experience, the term *néant* refers primarily to the multiplicity or relativity of all human values. There is no single truth which underlies or inspires human endeavors. Carried to the extreme, the concept of *le néant* can lead to the conclusion that all actions are equally insignificant or absurd. Spiritual certitude, like the Symbolists' attitude toward the exterior world or the despairing lassitude of the aging politician Lambert de Besme in Claudel's *La Ville,* becomes irrevocably fragmented. God, who in such a context is simultaneously everywhere and nowhere, has no absolute authority and no definitive answers. He can offer only multiple truths which, being in themselves incomplete, cannot fulfill human needs and therefore leave individuals in a state of constant agitation or constant desire.

Rivière could not accept just one form of truth when faced with what he felt were so many possibilities to explore. This attitude, coupled with the pleasure he derived from his nervous tension, kept him from accepting Claudel's suggestions about how to find peace and spiritual health. Claudel's answers seemed too simplistic for Rivière. Seeing all the different resources of his own being and of the world around him to be examined and developed, he could not close his eyes to them and, as Claudel urged, submit to the discipline of the Catholic Church. Though Rivière admitted the depths of his egoism, he rejoiced in the very admission of this attitude and refused to relinquish anything of himself, no matter how confused he was at the time.

During the summer of 1907, Rivière struggled with, or more precisely against, the force of Claudel's counsel, which he had so earnestly sought out earlier that year. Claudel offered nothing Rivière could accept without making an irremediable choice. Put off by Claudel's domineering tone and unqualified certitude, he soon realized that their attitudes were irreconcilable. Rivière really did not want Claudel to abandon him, and he sincerely sought to present an accurate interpretation of Claudel's vision in his article for *L'Occident,* but the young man also considered this work to be a parting tribute to the author who had shaken him from his adolescent lethargy. Unsatisfied by the nature of his encounter with Claudel, Rivière had to search elsewhere for answers. As he explained to Gabriel Frizeau in November 1907: "I made a great sincere effort. It didn't succeed. I can't help it. Besides I never felt so far from all Christianity."[18] And in other letters to Frizeau over the next six months Rivière continued to stress the enormous gulf between himself and religious orthodoxy. The situation seemed to him beyond all hope of salvation.

It is important to note, however, that although Rivière fled beyond Claudel's reach and discovered another form of personal certitude in his relationship with Isabelle Fournier, the two men did continue to correspond for several more years. During this period from late 1907 up to the War, their letters gradually decreased in number and changed in subject matter. They dealt more and more exclusively, on the one hand, with purely philosophical and literary topics or, on the other, with practical matters, such as Rivière's impending marriage and choice of a career. But despite the apparent spiritual distance between them, the lines of communication and indirect influence were kept open.

It is equally significant that in his letters to Fournier during the same prewar period, Rivière continued to wrestle quite openly with religious problems. He in no way abandoned his struggle. Despite his insistence that he would never be a Catholic, he never completely rejected this possibility. As his numerous comments on spiritual issues to Fournier over this six-year period indicate, his original objections to Catholicism and his refusal to accept it gradually diminished in magnitude and scope. In 1909, for example, he told Fournier that he was still deeply tempted by Catholicism, but he could as yet not accept the simple explanations it proposed to resolve complex questions. The parts of the puzzle seemed to fit together too easily. Nor could he tolerate the sense of satisfaction in feeling that they possessed the truth that he noticed in certain Catholics around him—in Gabriel Frizeau, in another Claudel convert, the poet Francis Jammes, and even in Claudel himself. Rivière had already come so far in his spiritual evolution, however, that these problems were essentially the only major obstacles remaining between him and Catholicism. As he assured Fournier in May of that year, "This is my only objection. The day that this is taken from me I'll be a Christian. Nothing separates me so from Christianity than feeling myself too disposed to it. . . . I can't believe in original sin because it is a too profound, a too satisfactory explanation of the insufficiency in all things" (*Corr. R-F,* 2:288).

He was already much more restrained in his objections than he had been two years previously. And once he realized, as Isabelle Rivière points out in her introduction to the Rivière-Claudel correspondence, that the discipline of Catholicism was more difficult and more precarious for the self than other attitudes, very little serious resistance remained. By 1912, when he came to write the account of his spiritual struggle entitled "De la Foi," Rivière could justify and accept the doctrine of original sin, which had troubled him for so long, and the attitude he had originally called his complete *inability* to adhere to Catholicism became more simply the *difficulty* he had in believing. Though he would never completely resolve his spiritual problems once and for all and though his faith would always be a very private concern, Rivière would, for several years at least, enjoy an unusual period of religious exaltation. With the outbreak of World War I, he would finally experience the kind of individual encounter between "Him and me" which he had described to Fournier in 1907, at the time of his first letter to Claudel, as being so necessary for his *complete* conversion. He would also undergo the kind of personal humiliation he needed for the pendulum of his self-preference to swing in the opposite direction and enable him to outgrow his adolescent egoism. It would also help him learn to look at himself less melodramatically and eventually to develop the kind of open-minded moderation which would characterize his outlook after the war.

Chapter Three

Quest for Personal Autonomy: Rivière's Relationship with Gide

Rivière's Initial Encounter with Gide's Attitudes

Rivière's passionate commitment to self-development, his cultivation of desires for their own sake, his belief in the relativity of all values, and his need to live dangerously at a high point of emotional tension all coexisted with his yearning for calm and security. As we have seen, these tendencies toward psychological agitation and love of risk found encouragement and, to a certain extent, justification in the ego-centered works of Barrès and then in the ambivalent aspects of Claudel's early plays. But this self-conscious, highly individualistic side of Rivière's personality discovered its most fertile and most fascinating literary counterpart in the works of André Gide. Rivière began very slowly to discover Gide's creations in 1905 and early 1906, at the same time that he was first rejoicing in the primitive, sensual aspects of Claudel's plays. And Gide is the only author who ever comes close to rivaling Claudel in his long-term interest and admiration during the prewar years.

The first reference to Gide in Rivière's letters to Fournier is dated 4 August 1905, and it indicates his general confusion: "Yesterday I read a little of André Gide's *Prométhée mal enchainé*. I confess as to having understood nothing. I'll try" (*Corr. R-F*, 1:27). The next allusion to Gide, dated 5 November 1905, appears in the same letter where Rivière first mentions having leafed through Claudel's drama anthology *L'Arbre* in a bookstore and emphasizes how deeply it has already attracted him. This time he tries to describe his reaction to some of the individual pieces collected in Gide's *Philoctète,* and he stresses in particular "the incomprehensible and above all the intransmissible charm" (*Corr. R-F,* 1:106) of *La Tentative amoureuse.* In contrast to his initial contact with Claudel's dramatic world, which overwhelmed him almost immediately and about which he could soon discourse for several pages at a time in letters to Fournier, Rivière's first en-counters with Gide left him in a state of stunned suspension. Only when he began to read *Les Nourritures terrestres* in the summer of 1906 and to follow the wanderings of its enigmatic protagonist, Ménalque, could he begin to understand the structure of Gide's literary world and his own reaction to it. The heretofore inde-cipherable pieces of the puzzle slowly began to fall into place.

Born in 1869, André Gide was an extremely nervous, intro-verted child, the only son of a wealthy Paris physician who died when the boy was only eleven. Even before his father's death, Gide's activities were controlled for the most part by his mother, and her authority became all the more tyrannical when she had to accept full responsibility for her son's upbringing. Gide's mother was a humorless, unimaginative, rigidly pious woman who inculcated very early in her son an overwhelming sense of sexual guilt and an equally strong sense of filial duty. In 1893, at the age of twenty-three and after years of nervous frustration, he finally broke loose from his mother's stifling influence and left France for the first time to travel to North Africa with an artist friend, Paul Laurens. During the months spent in that desert land, Gide discovered the sheer physical pleasure of living and experienced his first homosexual encounters with the vigorous, suntanned Arab youths whom he would describe so vividly in some of his later writings. Temporarily at least he threw off the restrictions imposed by his mother and his puritanical unbringing and immersed himself in the strange beauty of the North African landscape, which he seemed to discover anew each morning. *Les Nourritures terrestres,* written in a state of intense physical agita-tion, constitutes Gide's personal manifesto concerning the importance of freeing oneself from the bonds of the past, struggling to be self-sufficient, and learning to live each day to the fullest without regrets. The trip to North Africa and the writing of *Les Nourritures terrestres* was an expression of revolt and independence which was absolutely vital to Gide's maturation process and without which he could have attained no degree of psychological autonomy.

When the young, naive Rivière read *Les Nourritures terrestres,* he eagerly assimilated much of what it had to offer. Confronted by the Gidean passion for uninhibited self-realization and the desire for perpetually new experiences revealed so temptingly through Ménalque's restless actions, Rivière reveled in the unabashed sensualism which the work expressed. He expressed his enthusiasm and admiration for the mysterious Ménalque, who, at the age of eighteen, severed all ties with his family and set out alone to pursue a life of adventure. As he had previously delighted in the delicate restlessness of Barrès's landscapes, Rivière likewise rejoiced in the very barrenness of Gide's desert realm and the intense degree of awareness required to survive there. This attitude acted as a necessary counterpoint both to the calm which he felt surrounded Bordeaux and which still influenced him and to the overwhelming richness of Claudel's landscapes.

It should also be noted that although Rivière was fascinated by the exotic qualities of Gide's descriptions and by the strange heroism of the Nietzschean-inspired Ménalque, he recognized the limitations inherent in Gide's North African landscape and in Ménalque's concept of adventure. Rivière was not taken in by Gide's hypnotic literary style. He clearly understood the superficiality of the work as a whole and of the attitudes it presented, but he also felt that the expression of those attitudes was vitally important. As he explained to Fournier, "Yes, it's true, Gide has nothing to say. But this very fact that he has nothing to say is something positive which needs to be said" (*Corr. R-F,* 2:13). Rivière knew exactly what Gide's highly autobiographical works had to offer. He had no illusions about the depth of Gide's world. Yet, at the same time, he understood more and more clearly how, at this stage in his development, he could profit from Gide's paradoxical doctrine where absence and thirst became states not only to be cultivated but actively pursued.

What is perhaps even more significant than Rivière's understanding of the terms of Gide's attitude at this point, however, was his insight into the relationship between Gide's universe and Claudel's, which he explained in his letters to Fournier. The two authors were diametrically opposed to one another in their conception of God and their reaction to religion in general. Nevertheless, their attitudes were in another sense closely related because, as Rivière stressed in mid-January 1907, "Gide's entire work is an almost necessary introduction to Claudel's" (*Corr. R-F.* 2:13). He understood how Gide's attitude toward passionate sensation and his frenzied search for an absolute in a fragmented world could be said to find its complement in the intricate, multi-leveled harmony of Claudel's cosmogony with which he was already quite familiar. Gide's dialogue with thirst, absence, and "non-being" could be interpreted as an essential prelude to and preparation for Claudel's exclusive commitment to the richness of "the Supreme Being" and his struggle to possess the earth while ascending to new heights of spiritual awareness.

Yet while admitting the loftiness of Claudel's inspiration in relation to Gide's rebellious dilettantism, Rivière also knew that Claudel's security was not for him. Although he continued to express enthusiasm for Claudel's literary creations and even sought to resolve his spiritual dilemma through personal contact with the healing power of Claudel's counsel, Rivière could not, at this point, accept that counsel. He drew back because of the very force of Claudel's suggestions and also because he was still deeply involved in the absorbing adventure of the search itself.

Rivière's Personal Essays and Letters to Gide

In his reaction against Claudel's prodding, however, Rivière did not go to the other extreme and become Gide's disciple, either, as has often been charged.[1] Many years later, in his open letter to the *NRF* responding to Henri Massis's vicious charges against Gide's corrupting persuasiveness and the moral laxity of the review's editorial policy, Rivière publicly explained once and for all the nature and the scope of Gide's influence: "Gide formed us all . . . but never, near any man, was it easier to become oneself as soon as one perceived one was different from him" (*NE,* 231). And Gide himself made sure that those who professed affinities with him recognized their own individual potential. It must be stressed that, like Claudel, he too wanted to inspire the young people around him, but the kind of influence he wished to exert was totally different from that of Claudel, who felt that his answers and his alone were the right ones. As Rivière further insisted, despite the charm and natural appeal of his aesthetic and his desire to be the center of attention, Gide in no way sought to force his attitudes on others. Instead, "He allowed each person the right to resist; if need be he even helped you in that resistance" (*NE,* 231). In other words, Gide suggested possibilities to the anguished young men of the early twentieth century and offered encouragement on an individual level, but he did not impose specific answers as absolutes or universals valid for all.

Rivière recognized that although he was in many ways very close to Gide, he, like Nathanaël in *Les Nourritures terrestres,* had to find his own solutions to the metaphysical problems plaguing him and map out his own direction in life. In order for them to be authentic, he had to discover his own kind of faith and his own reasons for believing. The narrator urged Nathanaël at the very end of the work, "Cast my book aside, tell yourself that it is only one of the thousand attitudes possible in the face of life, search for your own."[2] So also did Rivière have to continue his struggle alone. As evidenced by his correspondence with Fournier and perhaps even more so by several prewar letters to Gide which later appeared in the *NRF,* Rivière did not in any way abandon his dialectic with Catholicism in the period following his rejection of Claudel's advice and the admission of his attraction to Gide's ideas.[3] Since Gide did not try to make Rivière adhere to his own set of rules, a long-term friendship on a personal and professional level could develop between them as could never have existed between Rivière and Claudel because of the latter's zeal to guide lost souls back to the fold of the Catholic Church. Rivière soon found that he could speak much more freely with Gide concerning his changing attitudes and spiritual turmoil because Gide was willing to listen without condemning his ideas or pressuring him into submission.

Rivière's six published letters to Gide which span the period from March 1909 to January 1913 deal with literary and psychological as well as spiritual issues. At times Rivière simply elaborates on some of the ideas discussed at length in earlier letters to Fournier. For example, he reiterates his reaction to the limitations of Ménalque's attitude, reaffirms his continued belief in the equivalency of values, and reemphasizes the link between desire and happiness. But in most instances Rivière's letters to Gide offer new information and new insight into his developmental process as a whole.

In the light of Rivière's specifically *literary* evolution, the most important letter is the one dated 7 and 8 June 1912, in which he describes in detail the range of his abilities as a writer and explains that he will never be a novelist or "a creative writer."[4] As we have stressed from the outset of our study, Rivière's specific talent was critical in nature. Over the years he saw more and more clearly that "The realm reserved for me is the area of pure psychology . . . how at ease I feel when it's a question of comments."[5] He realized that he would succeed only with critical analyses or detailed psychological portraits.

Yet despite his clear insight into the nature and scope of his ability, Rivière would nevertheless give in to the temptation to try his hand at the novel. At this point in his career he was already so busy with the *NRF* that he had been forced to abandon work on an initial creative project conceived several years earlier and which was to have been called first *Bel Eté,* then *Les Beaux Jours.*[6] But, inspired by the example of his best friend and lured on by the urgings of Gide and others associated with the *NRF,* he would eventually make not just one but two other attempts to write sustained creative works. As we shall see in a later section, his efforts would be largely unsuccessful and would mainly serve to indicate the accuracy of his original assessment.

From a psychological and spiritual point of view, the two most significant of Rivière's letters to Gide are those of 3 January 1911 and 4 January 1913, in which he analyzes the latest changes in his continually evolving concept of sincerity and the current status of his religious attitudes. These two letters discuss specific issues not referred to in his other correspondence from the same period and must be examined in relation to Rivière's two important prewar personal essays "De la Sincérité envers soi-même" and "De la Foi," which reveal him as being closer than ever to Catholicism. With regard, first, to Rivière's attitude toward sincerity, it should again be noted that the opening paragraphs of his very first letter to Fournier in January 1905 already stress the necessity for being faithful to one's inner self. Rivière felt that above all neither he nor his correspondent should be afraid to reveal their personalities, for "By following one's inner truth, one is sure not to deceive oneself" (*Corr. R-F*, 1:9). The growth process which Rivière briefly sketched in this early letter constituted a reaction against arrogant, hypocritical literary sophistication, and, at first glance, his directive appears fairly easy to follow. Sincerity, it would seem, results quite naturally from remaining true to one's inherent characteristics. But as Rivière tried to define his often conflicting tendencies and then relate them to the concept of truth, the situation became increasingly complicated and difficult to deal with. In fact Rivière got so confused that for a time he tried to suppress altogether the whole problem of sincerity.

The next step in his treatment of the issue was to reject completely the possibility that any real truth or sincerity could ever be attained at all. Human life appeared to be nothing more than a series of masks worn to conceal a void. It was precisely at this stage in his evolution that Rivière asserted in his most disillusioned terms the all-pervasive influence of *le néant*, which reduced all human actions to the same level of insignificance. By 1908, however, encouraged by the two-sided harmony he discovered in Claudel's works, by the affirmative aspects of Gide's struggle for authenticity, and by events in his personal life (namely his relationship with Isabelle Fournier), Rivière fully recognized the error of such an extreme and basically counterproductive attitude. He was finally able to tell Fournier, "I am restoring . . . meaning to words I once believed void of all significance, such as happiness, truth, sincerity" (*Corr. R-F,* 2:24). Yet since his own tendencies were still so dualistic and since he could not accept the idea of an unchanging, universal truth, sincerity, too, could only be described as a series of continuous, though authentic, transformations—an attitude which again reveals his affinity with Gide at this point. It could only be defined as "the progressive description of truth . . . the succession of the perhaps contradictory avowals of an entire life" (*Corr. R-F,* 2:248). And it changed form somewhat existentially according to the terms of a specific situation.

As Rivière drew further away from Claudel's constricting dogmatism, recognized more clearly the basic differences between him and Gide, and began to stand more firmly on his own, he also discovered that even this dynamic, fluid kind of sincerity did not develop nearly as easily as he had surmised a few years earlier. In his all-important letter to Gide dated 3 January 1911, he describes in detail the specific nature of his difficulties with the whole problem of personal sincerity. As he explains to Gide: "I must work at my sincerity toward you,"[7] because true sincerity is not superficially spontaneous at all. It does not develop without considerable effort, for it is very difficult to be oneself under the often conflicting influence of internal and external pressures. In describing his own situation for Gide's understanding as well as his own, Rivière complains at length about his coexisting timidity and his persistent need to confess. These tendencies conspire to keep him from expressing what he really believes and thus keep him from being sincere and reaching the goal he so earnestly seeks to attain. The problem is made even more complicated by his need for approval which acts as yet another distorting influence. At the end of his letter he admits that he is still caught between his desire to express what he really feels he is and his compulsion to camouflage his authentic reactions, unable to reconcile these conflicting tendencies.

Rivière's own essay on personal sincerity which appeared in the *NRF* in 1912, a year after he wrote this illuminating letter to Gide, further elaborates on the complexities of this situation. The essay also proposes a rather paradoxical but ingenious way of dealing with the dilemma, which, in turn, reveals Rivière's developing psychological independence. In the opening paragraphs, he refers to sincerity as "a perpetual effort to create one's soul as it is."[8] Through this statement Rivière synthesizes comments made at various times in the previous six years and, most recently, in his letter to Gide. He again emphasizes the absorbing sense of commitment necessary to attain sincerity and the fluidity of the concept itself, once again revealing the influence of Gide's attitudes on his own. What is much more important, however, is that now for the first time Rivière spells out in detail the serious dangers which can arise from trying to be sincere and follow exactly the dictates of one's inner self—an explanation which reveals a new and important change in his evaluation of the problem and in the development of his intellectual autonomy.

As the opposite of superficial, instinctive spontaneity, Rivière's devastatingly lucid type of sincerity illuminates even the most obscure corners of the human personality with total disregard for morality. Contemplating these areas of the human psyche, however, is potentially dangerous. It can, for example, lead to the difficulty of attributing too much significance to the "soul's evil thoughts,"[9] in relation to less sensational attitudes or reactions. An even greater danger, in Rivière's eyes, stems from the all-inclusive quality of this piercing sincerity. It places an individual in direct confrontation with each one of his often conflicting feelings which he must maintain in equilibrium against the onslaught of moral or social repression. But in trying to preserve this delicate balance, he also risks falling into a state of complete psychological stagnation. The seemingly dynamic principle of sincerity can itself become yet another kind of restriction impeding personality development, for, as Rivière stresses, "The sincere man dare not touch his sentiments; he would be ashamed to change them, to modify the least one of them. . . ."[10] Any movement whatsoever would destroy his precarious completeness; thus the only option open to him is to remain immobile and, like Stendhal whom Rivière cites specifically in his analysis, contemplate the different facets of his own internal wholeness or perfection. This kind of lucidity and concentrated introspection can in turn be self-defeating, for they shut out all contact with the outside world, without which there could be no psychological reactions in the first place.

Faced with these extreme but nonetheless real possibilities, Rivière observes that the only way to deal effectively with the problem of *total* sincerity to oneself is to abandon it altogether as a completely undesirable and inhuman perfection, incompatible with the adventure of living. He comes up, instead, with a most effective compromise. Rivière concludes his essay by opting for the more down-to-earth, more realistic concept of well-proportioned intellectual honesty rather than the ideal of total personal sincerity, which can be as detrimental to human development as commitment to any other narrow absolute. Rivière still insists that "the truly honest man"[11] must openly admit to himself the existence of even his most morally reprehensible thoughts. But he must also keep a sense of proportion and recognize the primary importance of interaction with others so as not to become the prey of his own paralyzing lucidity, or like Gide, fall victim at times to using the concept of personal sincerity as an excuse to mask certain personal shortcomings.[12] As Rivière's sense of irony had helped him maintain control of his meanderings in the past, so also do his underlying passion for the unpredictable, day to day activities of living and his increasing commitment to the Classical principle of moderation keep him from dedicating himself to total sincerity and from losing himself in labyrinthine self-analysis. Guided by his growing sense of internal balance and by his need to assert his independence from Gide's influence, he is able to arrive at an integrated solution which accommodates all aspects of the human personality and amply provides for continued growth.

It is also important to note that though he understood the dangers inherent in the concept of total sincerity on a personal level, Rivière's intellectual fascination with the whole problem and, in particular, certain literary treatments of the issue would remain one of his lifelong preoccupations. He would always be interested in trying to define more precisely and more concretely the intricacies of this phenomenon which had attracted his attention from the very beginning of his career. Long after the publication of his article on the pros and cons of personal sincerity, he would continue to explore the strictly psychological ramifications of the issue. As we shall see in a later chapter, for example, both in his novels and in his analyses of Freud and Proust, Rivière would return to certain of the basic ideas discussed in his essay and in his correspondence ten years previously, expanding them and integrating them into his postwar attitudes toward literature and life as a whole.

The first of Rivière's two letters to Gide which provide unique insight into his psychological evolution treats, as we have seen, the problem of sincerity and relates directly to the essay "De la Sincérité envers soi-même." The second of these important letters, written in January 1913, must be examined in conjunction with Rivière's other important personal essay, "De la Foi," which had just appeared in the *NRF* a month before. This article is a highly self-conscious *tour de force* in which Rivière tries to explain his personal concept of religious faith, his reasons for wanting to believe, and his particular image of God. As Rivière himself emphasizes at various points in his account, he is not trying to write an apology. He is simply expressing his individual reactions to highly complex theological issues. For example, in the second section where he examines specific reasons for believing, he asserts that "I intend to describe only the very personal movements of my thoughts."[13] It is essential to keep in mind that he is writing only about his own reactions at a particularly precarious time in his spiritual evolution when he desperately needs to question himself and outline step by step the changes in his religious attitude. The essay is a statement of his own position and, in a sense, a working out of some of his remaining difficulties.

Perhaps the most striking aspects of the essay are precisely its subjectivity and lack of concern for the critical reactions of his readers. When Rivière fears that the arguments he is outlining may not seem terribly logical he merely dismisses the issue altogether. After presenting a particularly anthropomorphic description of God, for example, he simply states that if critics wish to complain about the overly human quality of his portrait, "Then I'll be anthropormorphic."[14] In the end it even seems as if the principal reason Rivière cites for wanting to believe is essentially the same as the reason why he has such difficulty accepting Catholicism. At the beginning of the section in which he deals with the depth of Catholicism, he summarizes the arguments which he has just put forth by stating, "Because I am unable to do otherwise I believe in a supernatural reality."[15] He goes on in this part of his essay to describe what he believes to be the psychological validity of Catholic dogma and morality as well as his enthusiastic response to them. And in the concluding section, where he discusses the major difficulty that keeps him from being a Catholic, Rivière asserts that "I cannot wish to be different."[16] As he had so often explained to Fournier and Claudel, he cannot bring himself to suppress irrevocably any aspect of his character. He cannot be other than he is, however full of faults that may be. Hence, both Rivière's reasons for and against religious belief are rooted in the same opposing tendencies which struggle within him. And the fact that Rivière uses the verb *pouvoir* ("to be able") in both statements seems to indicate that his reasons for believing and his spiritual difficulties stem from the same principle. He simply cannot envisage the situation otherwise and throughout the essay seems frequently to be talking in circles, unable to change direction and break free from the convoluted structure of his argumentation.

Given the subjectivity and the excessively emotional tone of his statements, it is not surprising that Rivière's article has little strictly theological significance. It is, however, very valuable as a psychological and intellectual document for understanding certain key factors concerning the way his mind functions. Rivière's remarks in his January 1913 letter to Gide, written in response to Gide's criticisms of the essay, complement and clarify many of the statements Rivière made in his article and further suggest the importance of this essay in his overall development. Rivière's explanatory remarks in his letter to Gide help us understand why he had to write "De la Foi." The letter provides a specific context in which to consider the essay and enables us to untangle many of its ambiguities.

Rivière begins by once again outlining the similarities and the differences between Gide and himself, while, at the same time, stressing the depth and openness of their friendship. He then describes his attitude toward philosophy and philosophical questioning, specifies the kind of developmental procedure he utilized in "De la Foi," and explains more calmly and, in our opinion, more convincingly than in his essay why he is so attracted to Catholicism. He also touches briefly upon his present lack of knowledge concerning Christ and the Gospels, a touchy issue which would become the source of heated public controversy between Gide and the newly widowed Isabelle, in 1925.

Rivière's discussion of his philosophical tendencies early in his letter is particularly significant considering the unqualified disgust he expresses for this whole area of study throughout his correspondence with Fournier and his criticism of philosophical argumentation in "De la Foi" itself. Now when confronted by Gide's comments on his article, he realizes that despite his subjective point of view, his own method of dealing with Catholicism is basically philosophical in nature; it stems from his need to question his surroundings and his reactions to them in order to explain the world satisfactorily to himself. As in other areas of life, Rivière's initial desire is to understand how things work, how they function as part of a complex totality. This general philosophical orientation also helps explain why Rivière had to struggle for so many years with Catholicism. He had to try to understand it for himself without external pressure and deal systematically with each of his objections before he could accept it.

His overall philosophical approach likewise indicates why he was so little interested in the person of Christ at this time. As he remarks to Gide, "I never had any idea of a direct conversion. . . ."[17] Rivière's approach to Catholicism took a hesitating, circuitous route, and any personal encounter with Christ or the Gospels could take place only after the initial essential questions had been resolved and the overall structure of its doctrines accepted. Rivière openly admits to Gide that though he is closer than ever before to Catholicism, "I do not have a feeling for Christ . . . a true love for Him."[18] But at the same time he also expresses his intense anguish concerning this very indifference, insisting that "It is impossible that this last. . . ."[19] He has to proceed slowly, recognizing that each stage in his evolution represents a decisive struggle but confident that he will eventually develop the personal fervor that he now lacks.

In the light of Rivière's explanatory remarks in this letter, the controversy which Gide opened up in the *NRF* after Rivière's death concerning his attitude toward the Gospels was, in our opinion, petty and, to a certain extent, demeaning for someone in Gide's position. In his contribution to the issue of the *NRF* dedicated to Rivière, Gide at one point refers to Rivière's 1913 letter and expresses his shock that the young man's theological attitude "took no account at all of Christ, whose teachings he almost completely ignored and didn't mind ignoring. And not only was he not terribly concerned about this, but believed that one could be a good Catholic and do quite well without it."[20] When assessing Rivière's religious attitude, Gide seems to have deliberately lifted the young man's comments out of context and attributed to them a meaning which Rivière in no way intended for them to have. It is as if Gide were indirectly striking out against Rivière, trying to undermine the young man's position. Needless to say Gide's comments provoked the wrath of Isabelle Rivière. In subsequent letters to the *NRF* she pointed out Gide's self-serving misrepresentation and refused to let him get away with what she felt were slanderous remarks. Gide eventually tried to explain himself out of the dilemma in his journal (see the entry for 12 June 1926), but his comments are not terribly convincing, and an unpleasant air of hypocrisy still surrounds the whole situation.

Along with indicating how he became drawn to Catholicism, Rivière's comments on his philosophical tendencies in this letter to Gide also offer what we believe are very important clues to the specific nature of his religious belief after World War I, another issue which has been a source of confusion and controversy. Rivière approached Catholicism through endless personal questioning, and the more questions he posed, the more he realized that Catholicism could encompass them all. Because of its emphasis on the primary importance of the three, broad theological virtues, Faith, Hope, and Charity, Rivière found that he could maintain a certain distance or personal detachment as far as practical morality was concerned. Rivière gradually came to see that, to a great extent, he could remain psychologically intact. He did not have to relinquish control over his personality in order to be a Catholic because, as he admits to Gide, "Christianity is a vaster entity . . . it extends much further. . . . I understand all the room that there is in it, all that it admits . . . and all that it permits me to bring with me."[21] He could still, for example, give in from time to time to the intense egotistical pleasure of intellectual contemplation. Catholicism did not impose excessive moral demands or restrictions on him and was broad enough to accommodate even this egocentric tendency.

These remarks to Gide on the expansiveness of Catholic doctrine help us understand the nature and quality of Rivière's religious belief later in life when he would openly cease to practice Catholicism and would refuse to discuss spiritual issues even with those whom he considered his closest friends. If, as Isabelle Rivière repeatedly stressed in her letters to the *NRF* and in prefaces to certain of her husband's works, Rivière never gave up Catholicism, then perhaps this letter provides at least one indication as to how his faith and his silence after the war could be reconciled in the broad, all-encompassing framework of Catholic theology. His comments in this letter to Gide help define the basic terms of that belief and will also help us better understand his attitude toward the relationship between moral issues and literary creation which would become so vitally important to Rivière in the early 1920s, as he championed the cause of the greatly maligned Marcel Proust.

Rivière and Gide's Literary Creations

At the same time that Rivière was struggling with his personal essays and outlining his spiritual changes in letters to Gide, he was also trying to chart Gide's own literary evolution and "to surprise this soul in love with its mobility" (*E,* 144). Rivière's lengthy study, entitled very simply "André Gide," encompassing all the works the latter had published to date, appeared in two installments in *La Grande Revue* in the fall of 1911 and was later included in his critical anthology *Etudes.* Given the fluidity of Gide's personality as revealed in his creations and the ambiguity which still surrounded his early emotional life and his sexual disposition, Rivière's study offers remarkably lucid insight into the subtleties of Gide's makeup and the continuity of both his literary and psychological development. In fact, as Henri Peyre stresses in a fairly recent essay assessing Rivière's critical contribution, both his article on Gide and his earlier Claudel study, "were the best to that date on those two authors."[22] Rivière recognized at once the direct and unusually intimate relationship between Gide and the various literary personae which figure in his writings. As Maurice Nadeau notes in his introduction to the Pléiade edition of Gide's creative prose works, "It is his [Gide's] work which expresses his true image . . . because he discovered himself through expression. . . ."[23]

Rivière knew that only by following the sinuous path of Gide's maturation process from the abstract, readily discernible textual restlessness of his earliest pieces to the more calm and unified narrative precision of the somewhat later *récits,*[24] could he decipher both the texts themselves and, at the same time, seize the struggling inspiration behind them. Rivière's article by no means constitutes an exhaustive, in-depth analysis of Gide's aesthetics, but he carefully defines the essential elements characterizing Gide's evolution to date. And his essay is still critically valid today, even in the light of later, more highly sophisticated technical criticism. Though general, it is nonetheless incisive and accurate in its appraisal of the nature of Gide's evolution.

In the first section of his study Rivière concentrates on the stylistic and compositional aspects of Gide's development. In particular he singles out the gradual change from the anguished, though voluptuous, instability of his early works to the calmer, more even pace of his later creations. In *Les Cahiers d'André Walter, Le Voyage d'Urien,* and *Les Nourritures terrestres* the language is general and abstract and the stylistic development of the text is extremely hesitant, as if the author were unsure of the direction its next move would take. The originality of these works springs, in Rivière's eyes, not from unusual images or multi-leveled connotations, but from the endless variety of rhythmic forms which the clauses and sentences as a whole reveal—similar to the everchanging scenery which Ménalque discovered in North Africa.

With the publication of *L'Immoraliste* in 1902, however, Gide enters a new stage in stylistic evolution. The vocabulary in this work becomes both more precise and more concrete, describing very specific events or individual reactions to exterior phenomena, and the rhythm becomes smoother and more certain of its path, leading toward a definite conclusion or denouement. Along with outlining the stylistic changes in Gide's works, Rivière also analyzes the more precisely structural or strictly compositional aspects of Gide's evolution from the totally self-contained, Symbolist-inspired meditations of *Les Cahiers d'André Walter* to the more essentially narrative structure revealed for the first time in *L'Immoraliste*. In this work, for example, each chapter contains some element of progress or some kind of episodic evolution in relation to the previous section, however slight that development might be.

It is also very important to note that in *L'Immoraliste* Gide finally begins to relinquish a little of his personal control which directs the protagonist. To a small extent at least, Gide lets the protagonist Michel' lead him, the author, through the various stages of his awakening and transformation. As Rivière puts it, for the first time Gide "is absorbed by the characters whom he creates . . ." (*E,* 166). He is interested in them as entities somewhat different from and separate from himself, and he seems to step back a little and let them move more freely on their own than he had in his earlier works where the relationship betwen him and his characters was one of intense self-identification. For the first time in Gide's works it is possible to distinguish a definite distance between him and his characters—a phenomenon which adds a new dimension of precisely human interest and a new level of complexity to his development.

In the second section of his study on Gide, Rivière concentrates upon the psychological or specifically attitudinal changes which correspond to the textual development elaborated on in the first part of the essay. His most original comments in this section are those directly related to the changes in Gide's sense of personal isolation or his "subtle separation from the world . . ." (*E*, 174). Rivière painstakingly outlines the very gradual evolution of Gide's attitude toward detachment from the world and the people around him. First he deals with the way in which Gide expresses his isolation from others through his various characters. Initially his detachment takes the form of André Walter's fearful timidity: Walter shrinks from all human contact and is so bound up by his internal ambivalence that he has no idea how to translate his potential into action. In the next stage of Gide's development this timid detachment evolves into the passionate refusals of Ménalque in *Les Nourritures terrestres,* who aggressively rejects all attachments and delights in the solitary joy of self-awareness and self-possession. This same attitude later manifests itself in a slightly different way in the sensual awakening of Michel in *L'Immoraliste,* who becomes so completely immersed in his own internal development that he makes his ill wife accompany him on his frenzied travels and eventually drags her to her death.

The expression of Gide's sense of detachment culminates in the sterile, self-contained asceticism of Alissa in *La Porte étroite.* Alissa stoically refuses Jérome's offer of marriage and embraces what she feels is the divine call to physical abnegation and spiritual union with God. In her effort to be worthy of her calling, however, she becomes the victim of her own idealized self-image. Alissa feeds on the knowledge of her sacrifice and on the steadfastness of her belief. But at the moment of her death, she grimly discovers the vanity of her self-denial, the totality of her solitude, and what she describes as "the atrociously bare walls of my room."[25]

After outlining the way in which Gide's various protagonists express their different kinds of isolation, Rivière turns his attention to Gide's latest work to date, entitled *Isabelle.* He devotes a separate subsection to this work because in his eyes it is the most ambiguous of Gide's creations, seeming both to mark the end of one period and the beginning of a significant new stage in Gide's development. *Isabelle,* although in many respects more a literary exercise than a deeply serious undertaking, reveals a definite change in Gide's attitude toward detachment in two important and complementary ways. The characters, although still rooted in Gide's own psyche, are for the first time truly distinct, even though still only two-dimensional, entities. The initial inklings of character autonomy first revealed in *L'Immoraliste* are much more pronounced in this work, and the psychological distance between Gide and his characters is decidedly greater. At the same time, Gide also appears to be shaking off his cocoon of self-imposed isolation or detachment from reality, manifested in the actions of his earlier protagonists. As Rivière emphasizes, "He is coming out of himself . . . he is forgetting himself, he is losing himself a bit in the world; a kind of compassion attaches him to lives other than his own" (*E,* 197). At the same time that he is loosening his grip on his characters, Gide is becoming more interested in them as individuals and in the possibilities *around* him, rather than simply those within himself, another phenomenon which reveals a promising new dimension to his literary evolution.

In the concluding section where he summarizes his personal reaction to Gide's vision, Rivière again stresses the overall autonomy or self-sufficiency of Gide's psyche and, most of all, "the fidelity of his soul to itself " (*E,* 198). In this respect, Gide exemplifies the kind of sincerity which Rivière described in his personal essay which he was working on at approximately the same time he was writing his critical article on Gide's evolution. Gide has struggled "to create his soul as it is,"[26] and can legitimately be proud of the integrity of his personality. Yet since he also risks falling victim to this very lucidity and self-sufficiency, Rivière is delighted that, as evidenced by his literary evolution, "Gide is unhappy with his contentment, he feels the flaw in it" (*E,* 205). He will not, in Rivière's opinion, become paralyzed in self-contemplation as did Stendhal. Although Rivière cannot predict the direction that Gide's continuing evolution will take, it is clear to the young critic that Gide is just starting to develop his truly human qualities through interaction with the world and his abilities as a narrative writer by establishing a definite distance between his characters and himself. His future works will offer even more surprises, and Rivière hopes that eventually they will reveal an equilibrium similar to that of the *honnête homme* whose characteristics he was outlining in his essay on sincerity. Although Gide's literary vision is not specifically Christian in orientation and although it lacks the spiritual depth so evident in Claudel's works, it nevertheless encourages the kind of individual growth which is so necessary for responsible decision-making in a way that Claudel's never could. It is precisely this quality which Rivière admired so much in Gide. The example of Gide's method helped Rivière himself work out of his own metaphysical confusion and, moreover, to develop the openness and intellectual discipline that would characterize his critical writings as well as his editorial activities during the years of his commitment to the *NRF*.

It must also be stressed that Rivière's analysis by no means constitutes an unreserved panegyric to Gide's literary abilities. It reveals quite clearly, though subtly, the limitations of Gide's imagination as expressed in the works he had published to date and the inadequacies of his *récits* as works of narrative fiction. Through his study of Gide's evolution, Rivière reveals the finesse of his own critical capacities, while he once again affirms his intellectual independence and asserts his personal autonomy with respect to the force of Gide's influence.

On reading Rivière's article, Gide, for his part, was quite surprised and hurt by Rivière's well-received analysis. As Kevin O'Neill comments in his perceptive, well-documented monograph on Gide and the concept of the adventure novel, *To Gide*, Rivière's article was, "the last straw: now Rivière had joined those who had lauded his criticism at the expense of his fiction. Much affected by this partial betrayal and the implicit challenge it conveyed, he departed for Switzerland to cure himself of " 'this fluctuation, this indecision of my entire being' to which Rivière had referred in his study."[27] Just as Rivière had been influenced by Gide, so too was Gide, the established writer, profoundly affected by the keenness of the young man's insight and the directness of his comments. Gide knew that Rivière was basically correct in his assessment and had to escape temporarily from Paris so that the wound to his ego could heal and he could think about the direction he wished his future writing to take. Rivière's comments had hit home, and the young man's ever-developing influence with the *NRF* caused Gide to retreat and reexamine his own situation.[28]

In a much later study of Gide's evolution, presented as lectures in 1921 and eventually published in 1926 in *Les Chroniques des Lettres Françaises,* Rivière is more openly critical in his assessment of Gide's overall importance than he had been in his earlier article and explains in detail the reasons for his disappointment. Using the same general chronological classification that he had developed for his earlier analysis, Rivière again emphasizes, but in much more caustic terms, the stylistic and psychological instability of Gide's first creations, the superficiality of his youthful realm of sensual delights, and the dangerously tempting quality of his attitude toward travel and adventure. Rivière also stresses once again the limitations of all of Gide's narrative works, concentrating in particular on the desire for personal fulfillment that characterized the lives of both Michel and Alissa. Despite the apparent opposition between the paths they chose to follow, they were both animated by the obsession to sever all ties with the exterior world in order to follow the dictates of, on the one hand, an interior demon or, on the other, the belief in a divine calling to ascetic perfection.

When discussing *Les Caves du Vatican* and *La Symphonie pastorale,* published in 1913 and 1918, respectively, Rivière's comments become even more negative. In his remarks concerning *Isabelle* in his earlier article, he had emphasized his delight in the fact that Gide was finally beginning to relinquish some of his control over his characters, allowing them to develop more spontaneously, and Rivière had hoped that Gide would continue to progress along these lines. With his very next publication, however, Gide seemed to put an end to the aspirations Rivière had for him as a novelist. In *Les Caves du Vatican,* Rivière detects no element of textual spontaneity whatsoever. Lafcadio, like his very earliest predecessors, is totally cut off from the outside world, and the at times outlandish episodes follow one another in a completely artificial fashion. There is no structural continuity or inner coherence to the work. As Rivière stresses, "There are few works which are born from such a gratuitous design and whose details are organized with a more amusing arbitrariness."[29] To Rivière's extreme disappointment, the work adds nothing really new to Gide's repertoire, and the fact that Gide himself decided to call it a *sotie,* an openly satirical work with two-dimensional characters, instead of a novel, as he had originally planned, suggests the level of his own dissatisfaction with the work as a whole.[30]

The same kind of serious reservations which Rivière felt concerning the importance of *Les Caves du Vatican* apply perhaps even more strongly to *La Symphonie pastorale.* The work was treated by many contemporary critics as a caricature of Protestant hypocrisy, and Gide was quick to reply that he had had no intention whatsoever of presenting a satirized portrait. This reaction from Gide himself led Rivière to suggest that "Indeed it seems that it was by accident that the ending came to contradict Gide's principles and those of his hero,"[31] and to affirm that this sort of misunderstanding could have occurred only because of the basic instability and incoherence of Gide's ideas. As with *Les Caves du Vatican,* the work ended up as something quite different from what Gide had originally hoped it would be and only served further to emphasize his limitations in the area of narrative fiction. On the one hand it indicates Gide's inability to carry a narrative project through to a cohesive whole, and, on the other, it seems to illustrate an idea Gide himself developed in his lectures on Dostoevsky, where he stressed that "The novelist must not have ideas independent from those of the characters whom he has taken it upon himself to depict."[32] Gide's minister in *La Symphonie pastorale* ends up in a wretched state of spiritual disintegration. It follows, Rivière feels, from Gide's own comments on Dostoevsky that "Gide wanted to paint him [the pastor] as mediocre. . . ."[33] Hence, as Rivière bitterly concludes the first part of his presentation, "It is quite natural that his success be mediocre or nonexistent."[34]

In analyzing Gide's importance as a critic in the second part of his analysis, Rivière is nearly as negative in his appraisal of this aspect of Gide's inspiration as he was in his assessment of his creative works. He does praise the broadness of Gide's attitudes, the importance of his refusal to accept a limited perspective at a time when so many writers had fallen into the trap of narrow, nationalistic attitudes. Rivière also agrees wholeheartedly with Gide's broad, flexible definition of Classicism which "contains nothing restrictive or repressive."[35] But he concludes with the same observations concerning Gide's superficiality that he had first noted so many years before in his correspondence with Fournier. In describing the need for continual change which animates Gide's attitude, Rivière stresses, "We are touching here upon perhaps the fundamental trait of his character: an almost unhealthy independence, an absolute inability to be part of anything at all . . . this is perhaps the last word on his character. Gide is light . . . Gide doesn't weigh anything. He is on the surface of life."[36]

Rivière, however, does not end on this totally negative note. He softens the blow somewhat by affirming, as he had fifteen years before in his letters to Fournier, "It is . . . extremely important that in literature there are some minds or even only one mind which . . . perfectly detached, can come and go. . . . It is extremely useful [utile]that such a useless [inutile]mind exist, that no specific work either absorbs or distorts him."[37] And as evidenced by his open letter to the reactionary Henri Massis in October 1924 in response to the latter's diatribe against Gide's immorality, Rivière continued to value Gide's friendship and respect and the kind of beneficial influence which he could exert on those around him. Rivière appreciated having met Gide early in his career at a time when he was struggling to sort out the conflicting aspects of his personality and make his own career choice. He was grateful for the way in which Gide had helped, not only himself, but an entire generation of young Frenchmen discover and develop their individual capabilities.

After World War I when Rivière took charge of the *NRF*, his relationship with Gide became very strained. As we shall see in greater detail later, the two men disagreed about certain ideological principles involving the running of the *NRF*. They also became involved in an intense power struggle with Rivière trying to assert his authority as director and Gide attempting to undermine Rivière's control by criticizing the younger man's editorial policies in the pages of the *NRF* itself. The tension between the two reached a high point in 1920–1921. But by the next year, they were able to work out their difficulties to their mutual satisfaction, and their relationship improved immensely.[38]

Rivière prepared what was to be his last article on Gide's works during this troubled time in their friendship, and their deep personal disagreements no doubt inspired some of the rancor which surfaced in his analysis. But even though Rivière's article is bitingly aggressive in tone, it is still very valuable from a literary point of view, and the severity of its criticism could rightfully be considered as yet another mark of the depth of Rivière's feeling for Gide. It is precisely because he was dealing with someone who had so much potential and about whom he cared so much that Rivière felt so frustrated. Gide was not simply another writer to Rivière, but a profoundly gifted friend who, in the early 1920s, seemed to have settled for mediocrity and repetition in his literary creations. During the years immediately following the war, Gide seemed to be floundering in a state of literary limbo, unsure of himself and of the direction he wished to take. Judging from what Gide had written up to that point, Rivière felt that, after the publication of *Isabelle,* Gide had not gone on to develop his abilities as a novelist in any significant way. He seemed to have betrayed the rich promise of his earlier works, which had so inspired Rivière in his own developmental years. Rivière and Gide were able to satisfactorily resolve their personal conflict to the point where Rivière enthusiastically and unreservedly defended Gide against Massis's attacks. And if he had lived long enough to see the publication of *Les Faux-Monnayeurs* in 1926, the one work which Gide himself described precisely as a novel, it is quite possible that Rivière would have been able to look more favorably upon Gide's overall literary development as well.

Chapter Four

Commitment to Excellence: Rivière's First Years with the *NRF*

Organization of the *NRF*

No evaluation of the rapport which existed between Rivière and Gide prior to World War I can be considered adequate without discussing the complicated origins of the *NRF* and Rivière's important role during even the review's earliest days. This in turn will enable us to understand and assess the value of the articles Rivière contributed to the *NRF* during the first several years of its existence and of Rivière's critical method in general. The first issue of the review, inspired by André Gide and directed by the editorial committee of Jean Schlumberger, Henri Ghéon, and Jacques Copeau, came out in March 1909.[1] In his detailed and painstakingly documented analysis dealing with the beginnings of the *NRF*, Auguste Anglès indicates that in the early years of the twentieth century, Gide, surrounded by an ever-growing group of energetic young admirers, "dreamed of a collaborative effort in creation as Claudel, Jammes, and Frizeau had in prayer."[2] After years of fermentation, planning, and hesitation, the project was eventually launched. From the very beginning the *NRF* was bold in its revolt against the extremes of lingering nineteenth-century Romanticism and Symbolism and in its dedication to complete artistic independence free from all ideological and moral censure. The organizers of the review did not want to destroy all ties with the past as would the Dadaists after the war, but rather tried to arrive at and maintain a dynamic equilibrium between tradition and modernity.

It is also important to note that in their desire to emphasize aesthetic independence and creative autonomy, the *NRF* collaborators did not go to the other extreme and fall victim to the narrow Parnassian-inspired principle of art for art's sake. Nor did they in any way advocate a dilettante approach to literary creation. The *NRF* organizers were committed to what Schlumberger described as a twentieth-century version of the project of reform and renewal which Joachim Du Bellay had outlined in his monumental *Défense et Illustration de la langue française* nearly 400 years earlier. They did, however, refuse to judge artistic value on the basis of a priori moral directives and thus opened themselves up to the invectives of traditionalists like Claudel, who frequently objected to *NRF* articles and railed against what he saw as nothing more than another sign of the growing spiritual anarchy of his age.[3]

In the waning years of the nineteenth century, the would-be founders of the *NRF* had been addicted to the self-conscious attitudes expressed in Symbolist poetry, and they fully recognized that they had reached an aesthetic impasse. They knew that they had to search elsewhere for a more inclusive and down-to-earth set of guidelines which would enable them to confront reality, not flee from it as their predecessors had done. They could no longer adhere to the narrow exclusivity of any one particular literary philosophy; therefore they struggled to develop a coherent yet flexible framework which could accommodate many different viewpoints.

Inspired by Gide's concern for authenticity and his renewed interest in dealing with practical issues, the group of authors who gathered around him collectively sought to concretize their noble ideal of tolerance and broad-mindedness.[4] Despite their divergent opinions concerning specifics, they were unified by their assessment of Symbolism, their general conception of what literature was, their commitment to aesthetic quality, and their belief in the artist's role in relation to the growing fragmentation of the twentieth century. As Jean Schlumberger emphasized in the introductory "Considérations" prefacing the first issue, the *NRF* organizers were drawn together by "a unity of inspiration under the most divergent forms, a unity not of tastes, but of method, not of genres, but of style."[5] In their view, literature was above all an activity which absorbed all aspects of the human personality. It was a way of searching for truth, and a writer had to be willing both to explore all options open to him in that quest and accept the responsibility for his findings. He was neither a seer nor a high priest isolated in an ivory tower, but, much more simply, someone who was trying to see the world clearly and then to offer his discoveries to others on a one to one basis.[6] Though the writers who founded the *NRF* were opposed to literary doctrines as such, they did agree on these general principles as the framework for their investigations and on "the necessity for a return to objectivity, to a clearer vision of the real."[7] They also insisted on the need for intellectual discipline and stylistic rigor on the part of both creative author and critic if the review was to live up to its ideal of literary renewal. As Gide himself emphasized in reference to the problems surrounding the original first issue, they must not confuse irresponsible license with true aesthetic liberty.

Since their task was to be a collective effort, the *NRF* organizers also stressed the importance of group cooperation, which could at times run counter to strictly personal interests. Guided by an open-minded concern for truth and literary excellence, the various members of the *NRF* team tried to maintain a delicate balance between their individual concerns and those of the group without compromising either. They strove to present as honest and as broad a view as possible of current artistic and social issues and eagerly encouraged the participation of young, inexperienced, and totally unknown authors, such as Jacques Rivière. He first learned of the prospective publication at a dinner party in October 1908 and discussed the *NRF* project with Gide at their first meeting several weeks later. As he commented to Fournier soon after their conversation, "Visit to Gide-Schlumberger surpasses all hope. Gide, charming, simple, and talkative. . . . As it concerns me personally, inviting me to contribute to the *NRF*" (*Corr. R-F*, 2:260–61). At this time in his development Rivière had already drawn back from Claudel's pressure and he had already outlined his interest in and reactions to Gide's ideas in numerous letters to Fournier. Rivière's first face to face encounter with Gide, in December 1908, preceded by a two-year period of initiation into his writings, marked the beginning of an association which, despite periods of tension and frustration, would continue to develop until Rivière's death sixteen years later. Rivière felt immediately at ease because of Gide's unpretentiousness and was flattered by the older man's invitation to write for the new journal. For his part, Gide was equally impressed by Rivière's delicate sensitivity, by his earnestness and by his sense of personal commitment to literary excellence; he immediately recognized Rivière's potential and the value of his collaboration.

Gide's offer was doubly attractive because of the crisis Rivière was going through at the time concerning the choice of a profession. As his letters to Fournier clearly reveal, he was less than enthusiastic about the prospect of a teaching career. He dreaded the day-to-day classroom activity and felt that he was too timid to be a success with the students. Pushed into university studies at his father's insistence, Rivière detested academic specialization, and after receiving his *licence* he only reluctantly went on to prepare for his *agrégation* exams. When he took them and failed them in July 1909, Rivière was, however, quite shaken. "I had one hour during which I bordered on madness" (*Corr. R-F,* 2:313). He was distraught because of his sense of humiliation, but even more importantly because of the desperate bleakness of his financial situation. He was planning to marry Isabelle Fournier later that month, and he had no idea how he was going to support a wife. Through Claudel's intervention, however, Rivière obtained a part-time tutoring post that autumn at the Collège de Saint Stanislas in Paris and was able to eke out a meager living for himself and his young bride while continuing to devote every free moment to his real passion, which had always been literature and writing.

From adolescence onward, Rivière wanted more than anything to play a decisive role in the intellectual life of his times, and even though he could not be a captivating creative writer, he knew that he could develop his keen analytical skills to the fullest. When he wrote to Claudel about his career preferences, long after they had grown apart on theological issues, Claudel reacted with his characteristic assertiveness. He thoroughly opposed Rivière's intention to earn a living by his writing and urged him to opt for the much more sensible choice of *lycée* instructor. His first responsibility was to his wife and the family he would eventually have. With this steady source of income as security, he would still have some free time to devote to literary studies as an intellectual hobby. Claudel also felt that even if Rivière were fortunate enough to obtain a position with an important literary review, such as the *NRF,* he would lose his independence and eventually his integrity. "If you have enormous good luck, you'll enter a large journal where you will have to write not what suits you, but what suits the two masters to whom you give yourself . . . the employer and the public."[8]

From this sort of comment it would seen that Claudel lacked confidence in Rivière's determination and, more seriously, in his ability to maintain his intellectual autonomy under the influence of external pressure. Claudel was genuinely concerned both for Rivière's rather delicate physical health and his spiritual welfare, and he also recognized the potential dangers of the profession. But, as was the case with strictly religious problems, in this instance, too, Claudel did not really understand the person whom he was counseling. He did not comprehend the depth of Rivière's motivation and the strength of his personal commitment to a career as a critic. Despite the theoretical soundness of the solution he proposed, Claudel could not see that it was impossible for Rivière. And his statement about the intellectual servitude of the critic is particularly ironic in the light of Rivière's actual accomplishments during the years of his association with the *NRF* as contributor, secretary, and eventually director.

As we shall see more clearly later, Rivière never yielded to outside influences, and in the face of all opposition he actually *lived* the ideal of responsible intellectual freedom on which the review was founded. Just as he was drawn to Catholicism because of the vast, accommodating quality of its theology, so too was

Rivière attracted to the broad, all-encompassing aspect of the *NRF*'s principles, and he soon became a guiding force in establishing and upholding its reputation for critical excellence.

Rivière's Initiation into the *NRF* Circle; His Article on Dreams

During the first five years of its existence, Rivière wrote regularly for the *NRF,* contributing numerous critical analyses as well as several personal pieces, including two of his childhood-inspired meditations and a description of an exhilarating train trip through Champagne entitled "Voyage à Reims." From the very start, Rivière gained the affection and respect not only of Gide, but of the entire editorial team. By the summer of 1909, "He was already considered one of the group."[9] During the following winter, "[Gide] himself, Copeau, Schlumberger, and the others resolutely adopted this young recruit."[10] In his all-inclusive analysis of the *NRF*'s activities during its early years, Auguste Anglès repeatedly refers to the outstanding quality of Rivière's articles and stresses his importance to the project as a whole. Although Rivière lived in a state of almost unbearable nervous tension and became distraught at the thought of having in some minute way offended his elders at the review, Anglès is likewise careful to point out that "Whoever knows Rivière only by his mania for self-criticism would misjudge him. The adolescent with a passion for mechanical inventions remained alive in him."[11]

The same enthusiasm and intellectual acuity with which he confronted the marvels of early-twentieth-century technology, such as the airplane and the automobile, also inspired his attitude toward the artistic creations of the period. His ideas on the importance of moderation, clarity, and stylistic refinement corresponded closely to the ideal which the *NRF* founders so revered. Rivière had the unique ability of being able to synthesize the various points of view held by the members of the editorial committee. But it should also be stressed that he was not simply the *porte parole* for his elders at the review; nor was he in any way dependent on them for his own critical insight or limited by their impressions.

When Rivière came to deal with specific writers, artists, or composers, his highly individual kind of critical originality came into its own. Committed, even at this stage in his career, to the concept of criticism as an adventure in understanding the work or works in question and indirectly the consciousness behind them, Rivière entered into what could be appropriately termed an intense dialogue with the work to be treated, an activity which involved both emotional and intellectual reactions. He would then draw upon the discoveries made during the dialogue stage of his experience as the basis for elucidating aspects of its aesthetic composition. And finally he would synthesize his remarks concerning the individual qualities of the work into a coherent whole. In his effort to decipher the psychological and stylistic phenomena structuring a specific work, Rivière maintained his sense of proportion. Despite the force of his reactions and the intensity of his dialogue, he kept a certain distance between himself and the work being treated and did not exert deforming pressure on it. As Anglès emphasizes in his assessment of Rivière's critical method, "These objects are handled not from amateurish pleasure, but from the need to determine their contours, to measure their volume and density, to record their movement or to seize their immobility. Never lost from view, never deformed, they are surrounded as closely as possible, sounded as if with a stethoscope."[12]

It is particularly important to note that Rivière neither imposed his own preconceived definitions on a work nor lost his own identity in the dialogue process. But, in much the same way as Proust did in the realm of subtle psychological reactions, his intelligence sought "to fix the subtlest contours of the work in question and, at the same time, attain a kind of truth which goes beyond them."[13] Rivière examined works of art from carefully defined angles or points of reference, an approach which enabled him to focus his attention on specific elements within the works while never losing sight of the creation as a whole or of its role in the larger context of an entire career. And by respecting the uniqueness and the autonomy of artistic creations, he was able to produce equally unique analyses which both explain the works themselves and act as a reflector against which their brilliance can be measured.

Gide and the editorial board were so impressed with Rivière that they soon went even further than adopting him as a permanent, paid contributor. In December 1911, they asked Rivière to be the secretary to the *NRF*—a post he held until the war broke out, when the review temporarily ceased publication.[14] Rivière had already established such a firm reputation for critical sensitivity and personal integrity that, despite his youth, he became an all-important guiding spirit in the *NRF* undertaking. In fact, as Lina Morino notes in her general history of the *NRF*, even as early as 1910, "It could be said without any exaggeration, that Jacques Rivière was the very soul of the *NRF*."[15]

Rivière's very first important contribution to the review, like his childhood-inspired pieces, was a highly self-conscious meditation entitled "Introduction à une Métaphysique du rêve." Although it has nothing to do with metaphysics in a strictly philosophical sense, the text is nevertheless extremely important for what it reveals about Rivière's attitude toward dreams and the constructive, affirmative role they can play in man's psychic life.[16] Much like his developing attitude toward literary criticism, his concept of dreams was based on intense activity rather than on passive contemplation. As we have already seen, Rivière spent his adolescence and early adulthood under the influence of the Symbolists, who sought refuge from the world around them in delicate, distilled visions. Their attitude was largely negative in that dreams represented an elitist form of escape to a realm where they could indulge undisturbed in self-contemplation. Obsessed by the cult of ideal beauty, the Symbolists eventually became prisoners of their totally interiorized creations. As Rivière stressed in his analysis of the Symbolist heritage, "In the end there remained nothing more than a kind of perfume, an atmosphere, something which cannot be apprehended by the sense of sight or touch and which only the soul can discern and assimilate" (*NE*, 238).

By the time Rivière came to describe his conception of dreams in 1908, he had already outgrown or progressed beyond the narrow scope of Symbolist inspiration. Although his attitude in this essay is itself still highly interiorized or subjective in nature, what Rivière stresses most of all is the vitality, the richness, and the regenerating capacity of man's dream life. It is not a source of refuge or repose for exhausted intellectuals, but the realm of dynamic renewal. It is a kaleidoscopic world of spontaneous, energetic movement where danger is not to be feared, but met head-on and where the imagination is eager to explore hazardous situations firsthand. Rivière clearly understood the yet untapped potential of man's "imprisoned secret forces,"[17] which were struggling more and more insistently for recognition and sought to describe the kind of visions those forces could create in his introduction.

His meditation consists of two main sections, each of which is further subdivided into precise vignettes that specify the differences between dreams and what is traditionally referred to as reality. The most striking characteristics of Rivière's dream world are its vastness and the variety of its offerings. In the first section it is described as "the great marvelous country,"[18] where Rivière's imagination can roam without any inhibiting restrictions. This magic realm of seemingly infinite proportions is not without its own dangers. But despite the obstacles that materialize before his eyes and the phantom-like appearance of other voyagers whom he sometimes encounters, the dominant sensation is one of wonder, which welcomes the too-long suppressed murmurings of the subconscious. In Part II of his meditation, Rivière describes the difference between the splendor of his dreams and the sterility of what he describes as "the barren reality whose coldness now runs through me."[19] The fabulous visions of the night cannot survive in the destructive glare of the daytime world. Only in more primitive times could dream and reality coexist in harmony. The traditional concept of reality has been distilled to the point of complete evaporation. The well-ordered rational world no longer provides either incentive or compensation for the activity of living. Luckily man has other resources at his disposal. It is in the vast, more certain, and more vital realm of dreams that Rivière will seek psychic nourishment.

Rivière's reflections end on this note of energetic hopefulness. He is both convinced that his observations concerning the richness of dreams are accurate and certain of the impact they can have on others—an attitude which seems subtly prophetic in the light of future literary discoveries and affirmations. As Marcel Raymond is careful to point out in his landmark study *De Baudelaire au surréalisme,* Rivière's meditation is "a piece which is too little known and of a quasi-divinatory character, if one considers the future development of literature."[20] Many years before the Surrealists began their poetic experiments, Rivière emphasized the possibilities open to every individual through the exploration and cultivation of dreams. This kind of activity was, in Rivière's eyes, an enthusiastically affirmative undertaking whose ultimate goal was knowledge concerning oneself and others and truth. Rivière could not be considered a direct precursor of the Surrealists because of the basic difference which he felt existed between dreams and waking reality and because of the inner control and sense of ironic detachment he consistently maintained. In the course of the next few years, he would also focus his attention more and more exclusively on what he came to perceive as the richness of the exterior world. But he would never reject his belief in either the importance of dreams or the potential they offered for the benefit of oneself and others. And the ideas Rivière outlines in his introduction constitute an all-important intermediary stage between his adolescent, Symbolist-inspired inertia and the reality-oriented dynamism of a slightly later period in his development when he began to understand how the sense of adventure associated with dreams could also be found in the everyday world if one looked at it from a slightly different angle.

Rivière's Articles on Painters

After submitting this early contribution describing his personal conception of man's dream life, Rivière's attention turned more and more outward to deal with the many revolutionary cultural events taking place around him in Paris. During the next several years he wrote a series of short articles and reviews devoted to the painters and composers whose works were being exhibited or performed in Paris in the early years of the twentieth century. Since he had no formal artistic or musical training as such, Rivière's remarks must be treated as those of an educated, interested lay person who reacts spontaneously to the visual arts and to music on the basis of his personal preferences and then steps back to evaluate the accuracy of his initial intuition in the light of general aesthetic principles.

Rivière approached these forms of artistic expression with the same unique blend of personal involvement and intellectual rigor that characterized his attitude toward literature. Given the overall preoccupation of the *NRF* with questions of aesthetic form and Rivière's own growing interest in the richness of the world around him, it is not surprising that he concentrates above all on the individual artist's conception of and relationship to reality and the way these phenomena are expressed in his works. Rivière particularly admires those artists whose works reveal a delicate balance between sensuousness and intellectuality and who, through the power of their imagination and the skill of their brush, are able to capture both the form and the subtle movement of objects in the world around them, thereby inventing what could be termed a new image of reality itself. And the quality of his admiration varies proportionately to the degree of equilibrium evident in an artist's works.

Most of Rivière's articles on individual painters and his reviews of general exhibits have been collected in *Etudes* and *Nouvelles Etudes,* and our discussion will concentrate on those which, taken together, reveal the full range of his reactions and could be considered as the most representative of his aesthetic convictions. The artist who is the furthest from his ideal and about whom he is the least enthusiastic is Henri Matisse, because of the overly abstract quality of this painter's work. Matisse's creations are animated by the glaring force of his intellect. They may be clear and well articulated in form, but they lack warmth and human presence. He is so detached from the world that, despite occasional overtones of heavy sensuousness in his still lifes, he can be called "neither realistic, nor lyrical; he acts like an idea" (*E,* 42). His creations are the result of intellectual experimentation, not aesthetic transformation in which the entire personality of the artist is involved.

The dehumanized intellectualization which Rivière reacted against in Matisse reached a culminating point, in Rivière's eyes, in the sterile exercises of the Cubists. In his general critiques of the *Salons des Indépendants* in 1912 and 1913, Rivière spoke out against what he considered to be uninspired artisans whose problem was "not having any genius" (*NE,* 67) and who painted merely to experiment with purely theoretical notions. He felt that their works lacked any indication of personal authenticity, and he was deeply distressed at this destructive, antihuman attitude which more and more young painters seemed to be adopting. Although Rivière believed wholeheartedly in the autonomy of all forms of artistic creation and in the importance of the intellect in the genesis of a work of art, he could not accept the way in which the Cubists at this time seemed to reject all reference to exterior reality. He severely criticized their mathematical coldness and their lack of inner vitality which reduced the world to a bleak conglomeration of one-dimensional surfaces. He could see nothing positive in their pictorial analyses of abstract forms which neither offered a new definition of reality nor even broadened the already existing field of human experience. The Cubists whose works Rivière saw were not merely very detached from life as was Matisse, they were completely oblivious to it; their inspiration in no way equalled the theoretical boldness of their project.

In sharp contrast to both the mathmatically oriented Cubists and the detached Matisse, Georges Rouault seems to go to the other extreme and enter into direct combat with the objects around him. He tries somewhat frantically to subdue them in his paintings. He attempts to capture their essential form, in what Rivière describes as "an interminable struggle which never ends in triumph" (*E,* 44). Rouault needs not more suppleness, as does Matisse, but more firmness and control. This added constraint would, in Rivière's eyes, enable him to attain a greater sense of equilibrium between his emotional energy and his intellect, which, in turn, would make his works more aesthetically complete and more psychologically satisfying to the viewer.

The same desire to seize and depict the forms around him that inspired Rouault's effort also motivates Cézanne, although the latter does not grapple with objects in confused confrontation as did Rouault, but moves forward very cautiously; then, as Rivière indicates, "He leans over devotedly, he becomes silent in order to see better; he seizes the form which he reproduces in the circle of his attention . . ." (*E,* 36). Cézanne subordinates himself to the scene he is attempting to capture, and Rivière's only regret is that Cézanne has succeeded perhaps a bit too well in his self-effacement. Rivière would prefer that a transforming human presence assume a slightly more active position in Cézanne's works. In this essay on Cézanne, written in 1910, Rivière repeats, but in much more subdued terms, the same general criticism he made concerning the artist in the letter to Gabriel Frizeau dated 19 November 1907, in which he insisted that "What troubles me about Cézanne is his total abdication in the face of things, this exaggerated modesty and respect."[21] Cézanne remains too much of a painter in the narrow, representational sense of the term. And, in Rivière's opinion, it is Cézanne's extreme sense of humility which prevents him from developing his creative capacities to the fullest.

The artist with whom Rivière contrasts Cézanne in his letter to Frizeau is Paul Gauguin. Rivière feels that Gauguin actually transforms reality in his works. He is therefore "more than a painter [and] . . . he is a hundred times more moving than Cézanne."[22] Writing about Gauguin several years later, Rivière reaffirms and enlarges upon his earlier appraisal, describing how Gauguin is able to capture and bring out the aesthetic form or the symbolic value hidden in the exterior world. As Rivière puts it, "Under the power of his gaze nature takes on order . . ." (*E,* 47). Guided by moderation and an impeccable sense of proportion, Gauguin gently arranges objects so that the full force of their interrelationships are revealed and a new artistic unity created. Even though his colors may seem somewhat artificial at times or the luxuriance of his tropical scenes a bit overwhelming, the presence of the artist does not destroy the spontaneity of the vision itself, but rather seizes it and fixes it in another realm.

Despite his appreciation of Cézane's technical skill and his admiration for Gauguin's subtlety, Rivière found Dominique Ingres the artist who came closest to his ideal. Ingres's paintings represent for Rivière the most perfect balance between the emotional and the intellectual, the concrete and the abstract. Romantic fervor and Classical precision interact to reveal all the nuances of the exterior world where man plays a significant but not dominating role. Ingres does not laboriously force his subjects into submission, but rather, manages to capture the specific dimensions of their vitality. As Rivière stresses, "All at once he perceives the form which takes the place of all others; it is extraordinary. . . . But . . . it is accurate" (*E,* 34). And the simultaneously sensuous and precise lines of his figures depict the harmony he is able to see in the diverse objects around him. Like his master, the late eighteenth- and early nineteenth-century painter Jacques Louis David, whom Rivière also admires, Ingres looks directly at the world and transforms its often confused richness into finished, subtly balanced works of art, which involve the whole personality of the spectator. In a certain sense, Ingres's attitude could be compared to the moderate human ideal Rivière described at the end of his essay on sincerity, which he was already working on at the time he wrote his article on this painter. Animated by a keen enthusiasm for life while maintaining a delicate sense of proportion, Ingres deals justly and accurately with the situations he encounters. Like Rivière's *honnête homme,* Ingres "remains completely taken up with living, in a state of perpetual exchange, and engaged in conversation with the elements" (*E,* 36). And his paintings, which are both indicative of and inspired by this intimate rapport, have the potential to refresh and renew the vision of all those who come in contact with them.

Rivière's Articles on Composers

Rivière reacted to the visual arts with enthusiasm and subtle perceptiveness, but his passion for music was even greater and its influence on him more intimate. After failing his entrance exam to the Ecole Normale in 1905, he wrote Fournier stating, as he had grandly explained to his respected professor Mélinand,

"I want to study philosophy, I want to study music, I want to study the philosophy of music or even create a philosophy of music" (*Corr. R-F,* 1:25). Although he soon came to realize the difficulties involved in such a monumental project, Rivière's interest in music continued to grow. Music helped dispel the isolation he felt when alone in Bordeaux while his friend attended classes in Paris, and, to a certain extent, his interest in music rivaled his commitment to literature during the prewar years. More subtle and intangible than poetry, music expanded his perceptions while allowing his imagination to soar unrestrained. And the kind of music Rivière preferred at any one moment reflects, as do his literary tastes, the various stages in his development.

As he had stressed in his essay "Méditation sur l'Extrême-Occident," music "pursues beyond ideas the search for what cannot be conceived."[23] Music could bring one into direct contact with the unknown. And, in the early days of his career, Rivière, like most sensitive youths of his generation, completely succumbed to. the enchantment of Debussy's opera *Pelléas et Mélisande,* performed for the first time in Paris on 30 April 1901 and based on the play by the Belgian writer Maurice Maeterlinck. As Rivière, influenced by Claudel and then by Gide, gradually rejected the elitist weariness of the Symbolists and began to explore the world around him, so he also changed his perception of music and the kind of music he admired. The numerous articles on composers which he wrote from 1909 onward, the most important of which were included in *Etudes* and *Nouvelle Etudes,* reveal the nature and the scope of that evolution.[24] To a great extent they parallel and reinforce the ideas he stressed in his essays on individual painters, adding yet another note of coherence to his critical outlook in general.

Perhaps the clearest and simplest way to approach Rivière's complex attitude toward music is through his extensive remarks on Debussy. These comments, made over a period of several years, indicate the direction of his own development and easily lead into his articles on other composers. In the many references to Debussy in Rivière's correspondence with Fournier, in the articles devoted to Debussy himself which Rivière wrote for the *NRF* in 1910 and 1911, and in the sections on Debussy included in other slightly later studies,[25] Rivière always refers to the hypnotic effect which this composer had on his entire generation. Debussy's ethereal creations fulfilled their longing for a music that transported them into a secret realm "where the world was no longer anything to us" (*E,* 127). Rivière wrote to Fournier in June 1908 concerning the return of *Pelléas* to the Paris Opera, "I can say nothing other than the fact that never before or since have I been so overwhelmed. I experienced it with extraordinary simplicity; I no longer analyzed anything" (*Corr. R-F,* 2:224). The mystery of the work absorbed him completely. He could not sort out his reactions to the work itself or evaluate it aesthetically because he was too intimately affected by its magic.

Over the next two years, however, Rivière continued to make progress in his movement away from Symbolism. By 1910, he was sufficiently removed even from the reverberating effects of *Pelléas* to be able to analyze Debussy's creation, explaining why it was "the true masterpiece of Symbolism" (*E,* 129). But it is also important to note that by this time Rivière could see more in the opera than its Symbolist qualities. More and more concerned with clarity and aesthetic exactitude himself, Rivière saw that "there are many other things beside delicacy in *Pelléas*" (*E,* 128). Although predominantly Symbolist in inspiration, even this composition contained suggestions of another clearer, more precise kind of music that Debussy continued to develop and which reached a high point in his later orchestral poems, such as *La Mer* and particularly *Iberia.* This latter work was, in Rivière's eyes, more coherent and exact than anything Debussy had composed to date. Rivière was encouraged by Debussy's move toward greater textual precision in his orchestral poems and by the promise which this kind of evolution held for Debussy's future and for that of music in general.

In dealing with other composers during roughly this same period in his own career (1910–1913), Rivière expresses the same kind of aesthetic orientation and artistic appreciation that he did in his articles on Debussy and also in his studies of various painters. As was the case with the artists mentioned earlier in this chapter, Rivière is the most negative about those composers who, like Paul Dukas, are caught up in totally intellectual theorizing or those who, like Maurice Ravel, go to the other extreme and express only confused, indefinable emotions in their works. He greatly appreciates the subtle exactitude, purity of expression, and regularity of form that he finds in the compositions of Philippe Rameau and César Franck. But Rivière also emphasizes that these all-important qualities of textual accuracy and melodic continuity should be enlivened by the presence of spontaneous emotion, which adds depth and complexity to musical creations. For this reason Rivière is somewhat reserved about these two composers. He admires the formal accomplishments of both Rameau and Franck and considers their influence indispensable in the development of a more balanced aesthetic attitude, but he also feels that they are somewhat limited because of the extent of their emotional restraint.

The composers about whom Rivière is the most enthusiastic and who come the closest to his ideal of intellectual precision and emotional depth are J. S. Bach and Modest Petrovich Musorgski. Writing about Bach's *Passion According to Saint John,* at a time when he himself was still engaged in serious religious deliberation, Rivière stresses first of all that the work is "possessed by the thought of sin" (*E,* 112). It is both overwhelming emotionally and, at the same time, completely, even monotonously regular in form. It deals directly with basic spiritual attitudes; it relentlessly forces the listener to examine his conscience and confront directly the extent of his own shortcomings. It utilizes melodic repetition combined with ever-increasing psychological intensity to penetrate into every corner of the listener's consciousness with its lyrical force and its musical exactitude. It is impossible to escape its influence or to remain indifferent in the face of its revelations, for it is both an intimately personal creation and one which expresses the Christian sentiments of remorse and contrition. Struggling, as he still was in 1911, to work out his religious difficulties, Rivière responded passionately to the spiritual power of Bach's composition.

On the other hand, it was his continually increasing fascination with the unexpectedness of everyday life which inspired his enthusiasm for the Russian composer Musorgski, who, in Rivière's opinion, represents "the very soul of Russia" (E, 140). With infinite musical precision Musorgski delineates the intricacies of the human sentiments which he discovers around him and weaves them into a vast melodic tapestry that leaves the listener informed intellectually and deeply moved emotionally. *Boris Godounoff,* for example, is a dynamic, multi-leveled creation which captures the richness of life and transforms it into pure, carefully constructed melodies. It is, in Rivière's eyes, the very incarnation of musical plenitude, for its music is simultaneously mysterious and transparent, nonchalant and rigorous, turbulent and well balanced, and each quality comes through clearly. Rivière's most revealing and far-reaching comments concerning Musorgski are those in which he describes the energetic rhythm and the adventurous quality of his creations. "This music is all action. . . . It is surprise. . . . It is turned toward all things. It plays; it invents short, quickly moving stories" (E, 139). Musorgski seems to be continually looking around him, ready to accept any astonishing thing that might happen. He appears to be searching for new situations and sentiments while, at the same time, pondering how he can most precisely transform these phenomena into music which will tell the complete story of his native land and engage the total personality of the listener.

The same passion for aesthetic exactitude which Rivière saw suggested at times in certain of Debussy's creations, in Rameau and in Franck, and which he could discern much more clearly in Bach and Musorgski, reaches a culminating point in Igor Stravinsky's *Le Sacre du printemps.* He sees it as "an absolutely pure work" (NE, 73), and, even more importantly, the first masterpiece which we can place in opposition to Impressionism (NE, 73). Rivière's article on Stravinsky is his longest, most sustained piece of criticism on a composer. It appeared in August 1913, several months after the ballet's controversial opening in Paris. Rivière stresses the simplicity, the clarity, the precision of Stravinsky's creation. There is no turning back; musically it represents a complete break with the past and ushers in a new, dynamic, even violent era where what counts is the bold, direct presentation of well-defined realities. Above all, *Le Sacre du printemps* "is the renunciation of all extraneous things" (*NE, 73*) in both its music and in its choreography. Stravinsky rejects all suggestion, all subtlety, all nuance in order to concentrate his complete attention on essentials. Working in a carefully structured framework, he explores every aspect of those forms and announces in clear, crisp terms what he finds there. Similar to Musorgski, Stravinsky too "turns himself toward each thing and describes it, he goes everywhere; he says everything he must and in the most exact, the most rigorous, the most textual way possible" (*NE, 75*). Though Stravinsky is much more starkly intellectual than Musorgski in noting his discoveries, he, too, is an adventurer whose attention is turned outward. He perceives the richness of the resources around him, and he strives to transform them into surprising, startling musical realities which elicit equally startling reactions on the part of those listening to his compositions or attending a performance of *Le Sacre du printemps*.

Rivière is somewhat extreme in his emphasis on the musical and choreographical starkness of *Le Sacre du printemps* and, as Marcel Raymond stresses in his detailed analysis of Rivière's articles on composers, in his insistence that the work is above all a biological, mechanistic, prehuman presentation of rebirth and renewal.[26] But, in general, Rivière's assessment of the work's revolutionary qualities which inaugurate a new era in music once again attest to the accuracy of his perceptions. Moreover, Rivière's description of Stravinsky's interest in objective reality, of his musical adventurousness, and of his desire to fix reactions in clear distinct rhythms gives us two insights. First, it reaffirms the comments he made about Musorgski and finally, it prepares the way for his ideas concerning the evolution of narrative fiction which he developed in his most significant prewar study on the adventure novel.

"Le Roman d'aventure"

The three-part article entitled "Le Roman d'aventure," which appeared in the *NRF* in the summer of 1913, establishes Rivière's forcefulness as a critic of the novel and indicates the precise direction of his future development. In his excellent monograph entitled *André Gide and the Roman d'Aventure,* Kevin O'Neill explains the genesis of the idea of the adventure novel in France; he discusses in detail the development of the concept during the last decade of the nineteenth century and the first decade of the twentieth century with the writers who organized the *NRF,* particularly with Gide himself.[27] According to comments Gide made both in his private journal and in letters to friends, from the time he completed *L'Immoraliste* in 1905, he seriously contemplated writing an intricate, startlingly modern novel. Gide wished to publish the first French version of the adventure novel, and he also wanted to add another jewel to his crown as a critic by producing the definitive critical work on the issue, in which he would explain the particular importance of this kind of novel for the continued development of the genre in the twentieth century.[28]

Gide, however, was frustrated on both counts. In 1913, there appeared not only Alain-Fournier's *Le Grand Meaulnes,* but also Valéry Larbaud's *A. O. Barnabooth,* whose writing Gide himself had inspired and encouraged. In psychological complexity and narrative innovation, both of these far surpassed Gide's own work published the same year, entitled *Les Caves du Vatican,* which he had hoped would set the example for a new direction in narrative fiction. The second source of Gide's personal disappointment that year came precisely from Rivière's lengthy critical article, which was, as O'Neill has stressed, "the best piece of sustained literary thinking to be published by the review in its prewar years."[29] Gide was very much taken aback by the fact that Rivière had written this essay; the older, established author found himself upstaged by one of his youngest recruits, one who had already upset him by his subtly negative article published nearly two years earlier in *La Grande Revue.* Now, to Gide's even greater dismay, Rivière was revealing his own critical independence, not only in the pages of the review that Gide himself had inspired and done so much to organize but also on the precise topic about which Gide was the most sensitive.

In discussing the specific attributes of Rivière's study of the roman d'aventure, O'Neill emphasizes that, although it contained some original ideas, it was essentially a synthesis of attitudes and opinions expressed elsewhere. To a certain extent this judgment is accurate because many of the points made in the article are reaffirmations or clarifications of the principles behind the *NRF* and because Rivière does pull together diverse ideas in the air at the time. But the glimmers of originality which Professor O'Neill mentions briefly deserve, in our opinion, greater emphasis. It should also be further stressed that this article marks the definitive upward turning point in Rivière's career. It reveals his psychological independence and his boldness in tackling an issue so close to one of the most revered elders at the review; it demonstrates his ability to do a much better job analyzing a complex problem than anyone else writing for the review had been able to do; and it reveals the link between certain *NRF* principles and the ideas of other more flamboyant, more sensational avant-garde authors of the time, such as Guillaume Apollinaire. This complex study also provides the keys to understanding Rivière's postwar evolution and its role in relation to the earlier period of his career.

As Professor O'Neill notes in his treatment of Rivière's essay, the fact that he kept the word "adventure" in the singular, rather than in the plural as it had been used in earlier references to the genre, indicates the "new level of theoretical generality that was being aimed at."[30] Even more importantly, it subtly indicates Rivière's intention to write his *own* work. It establishes a certain distance between him and the *NRF* group as a whole. It also prepares us for the unique, multi-leveled meaning of the term "adventure" which Rivière develops in the course of his analysis, and it introduces one of the profoundly innovative aspects of the work as a whole in the light of the evolution of the novel since Rivière's time. The entire first section of Rivière's study and part of the second are devoted to explaining why a new aesthetic and a new kind of literature are necessary. People have at last turned

away from the psychological confusion and the stylistic inter-
mingling of forms that characterized the nineteenth century in
general. After decades of somnolence, the youths of Rivière's
generation are avid for the kind of hazardous encounters and
energetic activities which he had briefly outlined in his essay on
dreams several years earlier. The time is at hand when the potential of man's imagination can be realized in the exterior world.
No longer does reality seem to be bleak and monotonous, but
full of unexpected treasures to be gathered up and enjoyed by
those willing to search for them. As Rivière affirms, "In the
center of ourselves a new spirit . . . has begun to burn" (*NE,*
247), and this rekindled enthusiasm for life requires a new kind
of literature to express and satisfy it.

For Rivière the only genres which offered possibilities for renewal were drama and especially the novel. Poetry was much too
closely and exclusively associated with Symbolism in his mind
to be able to fulfill the changing needs of his generation. He does
not seem to have been at all aware of the profoundly innovative
efforts of poets such as Max Jacob, Pierre Reverdy, Blaise Cen-
drars, and especially Guillaume Apollinaire, whose Gargantuan
passion for life and continuously renewed desire for bizarre experiences greatly resembled the attitude Rivière himself describes
in his essay on the *roman d'aventure.* Apollinaire's anthology
Alcools, which came out in 1913, scandalized the literary world
with its inspirational and stylistic audacity by introducing a radically new concept of poetry; in many ways it responds to Rivière's
plea for a violent, energetic literature rooted in the adventure of
living in a surprising and at times disconcerting modern world.
It is regrettable that Rivière was not aware of the affinities between his attitudes and certain of Apollinaire's ideas, and that
he could not recognize the innovative potential of poetry—an
awareness which would have added yet another dimension to his
own investigations.

As it was, Rivière concentrated his hopes for change on the
novel. In the second and third parts of "Le Roman d'aventure,"
where he describes in detail the form which he hopes the new
French novel will assume, Rivière reaffirms and expands some

of the same ideas he outlined in his articles on individual painters and certain composers. For example, he again stresses the importance of stylistic regularity and purity that he noted when discussing Franck and Bach, and he repeats the need for a work in which the author's imagination goes everywhere in much the same way that Musorgski's and Stravinsky's creations do. It is also important to note that the interest in precision, clarity, and psychological plenitude that animate these composers are, in Rivière's eyes, the very principles which form the basis of French Classicism. In order to emphasize the rapport between the basic concerns of his era and the Classical tradition of the seventeenth century, Rivière briefly outlines the four steps in Descartes's method for arriving at truth as the immediate point of departure for his own detailed analysis of the new novel and the new novelist. Although a fiction writer will be guided by the combined power of his imagination and his intellect rather than by reason alone, as was Descartes in his scientific and philosophical investigations, he will, Rivière hopes, strive for the same kind of accuracy in his fictional creations that characterizes Descartes's writings. As Rivière indicates, "The imagination has its own rigor, a kind of unjustifiable evidence . . ." (*NE*, 258), and it is concern for this kind of perfection, coupled with the desire to depict actions and to describe accurately specific psychological reactions rather than merely suggest vague emotions, that will be the hallmark of the new French novel.

One of the most fascinating sections of Rivière's essay is his discussion of the intimate relationship between the novelist and the work taking shape before him. With his gaze focused on the world around him rather than on his own interior visions, the writer himself will be "in a state of adventure" (*NE*, 265). The very act of writing can be likened to a series of encounters with continually new unknowns. Somewhat like Musorgski and Stravinsky, whom Rivière described as turning outward toward all the objects around them, the writer will be constantly making new discoveries to incorporate into the complex construction gradually being assembled under the combined guidance of his imagination and intellect. He will be unsure of exactly where he wants to go until he actually begins examining and, in a sense, playing with his various discoveries. His own knowledge will develop inductively as he hesitantly transposes each psychological detail or single incident into words and then coordinates these with other already completed sections to create a satisfying whole. The work will be monstrous or gigantic in its finished complexity, much like Bach's or Musorgski's compositions, but each element making up that whole will have first been painstakingly delineated, thereby dispelling all possibility for confusion. Rivière is also very careful to point out that the new novel does not necessarily have to describe a sequence of events. The manifestations and connotations of the term "adventure" are numerous. Above all, "Adventure is the form of the work, rather than its subject matter . . ." (*NE*, 274). Both the writing and the production itself attest to the importance of initial uncertainty, spontaneity, and surprise. Whether the author is depicting incidents or the evolution of specific psychological reactions, what is important to Rivière is that the work bear the mark of the unexpected, which is, at the same time, the mark of authenticity.

In his manifesto for a new novel, Rivière is not advocating the kind of radical change in linguistic emphasis and authorial perspective that characterized the loosely organized group known as the New Novelists following World War II. He accepts without hesitation the essentially referential nature of the text, the necessity for linear development, the inherent accuracy of linguistic forms, and the overall passiveness of the reader, areas that have been under full-fledged attack since the late 1940s. But through his continuous stress on the textual aspects of the term "adventure", on the novelist's uncertainty about where his task will lead, and on the writer's curiosity to explore heretofore unthought of or forbidden realms, Rivière indicates some of the directions which later generations would take in their own reflections on the novel. His essay represents the kind of penetrating, antidogmatic examination that has been essential to the continued development of the genre and of literature as a whole in the twentieth century.

Rivière's article "Le Roman d'aventure" deals with broad, theoretical issues. As Marcel Raymond stresses in his treatment of the work, "Rivière knew very well that all he had done was to define a certain perception of life and to open paths to the novelist's imagination."[31] Nevertheless, the author who, during Rivière's lifetime, came closest to the ideal described in his essay was Marcel Proust. As Rivière himself would indicate in an interview with critic Frédéric Lefèvre in 1923, it seemed to him then that Proust's work concretized the theoretical position outlined in his prewar essay. As we shall see further on in our study, many of the key expressions Rivière used and the ideas he developed in the article would reappear and be reaffirmed nearly ten years later in his postwar lectures on Proust. Rivière's essay on the adventure novel represents, then, a major pivotal point in his development. It is a coherent synthesis of current literary ideas on the evolution of the novel. More specifically and more importantly, it clearly reveals Rivière's growing self-assurance, independence, and authority as a critic. It also links the two major chronological periods of his career and attests to the intimate correlation between his life and his writings, because Rivière's concern for precision, clarity, and open-mindedness concerning literary issues which developed very strikingly in the years immediately preceding World War I were also many of the same values that would inspire his personal conduct and guide his decisions as director of the *NRF* later on in life.

Rivière and Rimbaud

The last two articles Rivière contributed to the *NRF* before the war, sections from a lengthy study of the poet Arthur Rimbaud, appeared in July and August 1914. The complete text of this study, as it was written in 1914, was eventually published in 1930, whereupon it became the source of another complicated dispute between Isabelle Rivière and the *NRF* collaborators.[32] In many respects, Rivière's interpretation of the creations of the adolescent revolutionary, who wrote all of his poetry before the age of 21 and then disappeared into the North African wilderness, follows the same general direction as his articles on various painters and composers or his essay on the adventure novel. In this instance, too, Rivière concentrates on the kind of relationship which existed between Rimbaud and the exterior world and the way in which that phenomenon was depicted in his collection of prose poems entitled *Illuminations*.

At the outset of his analysis, Rivière describes Rimbaud's spiritual innocence and stresses the metaphysical quality of his revolt against the imperfections inherent in the human condition: "Being alive; there's the horror."[33] His poetry, however, is not simply the subjective expression of his revolt, the concretization of his private fury. Because of his very innocence, which separated him irrevocably from the human race, Rimbaud was able to discern "the image of a future reality,"[34] outside himself, whose form he alone could recognize. As Rivière explains in the second part of his study, Rimbaud's poetry is turned outward; it depicts a strange, disorienting world which, however, is not "another world, but this one in so much as the other disrupts it."[35] Focusing his attention on the intricacies of Rimbaud's disconcerting style, Rivière points out that "All his stylistic devices are those of someone who is examining something and describing it,"[36] rather than of someone who is concretizing subjective impressions, and he cites numerous examples to support his remarks. By comparing the working manuscripts of certain of Rimbaud's poems to their definitive published versions, Rivière reveals the tendency toward greater textual condensation, precision, and simplicity which, in Rivière's eyes, characterizes Rimbaud's evolution in general. Somewhat similar in this respect to *Le Sacre du printemps,* Rimbaud's poetry also represents a rejection of the past and a renunciation of extraneous things. He systematically destroys our fixed ideas and comfortable illusions about the nature of the world around us and offers us the outline of a new conception of reality which some would eventually call surreality.

At this time in his own development, however, Rivière gives a different interpretation to the discoveries which Rimbaud's creations depict so clearly. In the concluding pages of his essay, he meditates on the specifically religious significance of Rimbaud's disorienting visions and describes his personal reaction to

Rimbaud's works in Christian terms. Rimbaud's poetry has acted somewhat as a catalyst to Rivière's own religious evolution, point- ing the way upward and indicating the basis on which new spiritual relationships can be developed.

In contrast to Baudelaire's poetry which Rivière had earlier described as confessional and which stresses the intense relation- ship between the poet and the reader,[37] Rimbaud's works allow no such intimate bond to develop. The effect of Rimbaud's de- scription of a new reality on Rivière is quite different. His poems represent a door or a gate through which Rivière can pass into the realm of Christianity and where he can advance a little further each time he reads Rimbaud's works. Rivière was profoundly shaken by the radical nature of Rimbaud's descriptions, and, as he hypothesizes at the end of his essay, the wound which Rim- baud's poetry opened in his own psyche "can perhaps be closed only by the dogmas of the Catholic Church,"[38] whose all-inclusive qualities he had already noted in his correspondence with Gide (see Chapter 3, section II).

The value of Rivière's study as a work of serious literary crit- icism is greatly undermined by the personal, religious commen- tary at the end, which restricts the possibilities inherent in Rimbaud's poetry and masks much of its complexity. But the work does prepare us for the kind of intense religious awakening Rivière would experience over the next few years. Although he had formally returned to the Church, his faith was still fairly detached and impersonal; it lacked the fire of total commitment. Rimbaud's poetry represented, in Rivière's eyes, a general intro- duction to Christianity. In a similar way would the war disorient Rivière, catapult him into total solitude, and eventually enable him to ascend to spiritual heights through personal asceticism and meditation. Just as Rimbaud's poetry became, in Rivière's eyes, more and more condensed and concentrated, so too would Rivière himself undergo the same kind of compression, the same return to what he felt were essentials. The qualities he noted in Rimbaud's poetry indicate the nature of the experience he would undergo as he left his post as secretary of the *NRF* for the front in August 1914, setting out for what would become the most decisive personal adventure of his life.[39]

Chapter Five

The War Years: Spiritual Renewal and Commitment to Literary and Social Reform

Overall Impact of Rivière's *Carnets*

As the grim threat of war became more and more imminent in Europe during the summer of 1914, Jacques Rivière, like his friend Fournier and so many other young men, was called to active duty with the company in which he had served several years earlier during his year of compulsory military service. When Sergeant Rivière assembled with the other members of the 220th Infantry Division in late July, he began almost immediately to keep extensive notes describing the incidents, conversations, thoughts, and emotional reactions which in some way attracted his attention. In the course of Rivière's three years of wartime experience, most of which were spent as a prisoner of the Germans, he would fill more than fourteen notebooks with his varied meditations. These were eventually edited by his wife, Isabelle, and their son Alain and finally published in 1974 under the title *Carnets*.[1] The notebooks are much more open, intimate, and revealing than any of Rivière's correspondence cycles, even the nine-year exchange between himself and Fournier.[2] They bring to light the violently conflicting feelings and relationships he was trying to reconcile during this time away from family and friends, and they further reveal the continuity of his evolution. Rivière's notebooks treat in detail the private issues never before more than vaguely hinted at in his letters; they depict the terms of and the reasons for his spiritual transformation; they also discuss the various literary and political attitudes that would inspire Rivière's postwar commitment.

As Alain Rivière stresses in his brief explanatory comments introducing the notebooks, "Here, then, is the tapestry where so many essential threads of his life intersect."[3] They are the single most important *personal* document of Rivière's career. Since they have as yet to be examined in depth, we shall pay particularly close attention to them and to the important new information they provide, attempting to reveal the specific role which each of those threads plays in the tapestry of his life as a whole.

The notebooks were first of all the vehicle through which Rivière could understand and explain both himself and the events taking place around him. On a superficial level they fulfilled his desire for deeper knowledge of his own perfections and faults. More importantly, however, they were a lifesaving source of refuge, companionship, and psychological catharsis. Despite the diversity and the shifting nature of Rivière's comments, there are two psychological issues which, although his perception of them changes, run throughout the notebooks and give a basic coherence to the collection as a whole. The most obvious of these is the question of Rivière's personal conversion or spiritual renewal. The second issue, which in some ways is closely linked to his religious evolution, is his attitude toward two different women—his commitment to his Isabelle and his platonic, but nevertheless obsessive, relationship with a woman named Yvonne, which had tormented him for some months before his departure.[4] Despite his decision to end the relationship before he left for the front, Rivière struggled violently with memories of Yvonne throughout the first year of his captivity, and he was able to resolve the conflict only when he began to write about their experience, which enabled him to consider the whole situation in a larger perspective and recognize the limitations of this relationship when compared to his expanding union with his wife.

Yet another key in helping us to grasp the coherence of Rivière's notebooks and follow their evolution is a certain elementary, but nonetheless important, chronological division which parallels the most significant changes in Rivière's psychological and spiritual orientation. The period from the beginning of his captivity in August 1914 until the late summer of the following year, when he undertook an ill-fated escape attempt, corresponds to his initial, somewhat self-centered surge of religious fervor coupled with recurring and ever more haunting memories of Yvonne. This first year was the most difficult period for Rivière psychologically in that he was completely divided between his tranquil love for Isabelle and his troubled passion for Yvonne. He could not reconcile the two attachments and began his novel *Aimée* in a desperate effort to preserve his relationship with Yvonne and, at the same time, exorcise some of the anguish it inspired. The thirty-five-day period Rivière spent in solitary confinement after trying to escape represents a kind of turning point both in his attitude toward Yvonne and in his religious evolution. As we shall see, it was during this period that he completed the draft of his novel, which, in turn, enabled him to separate himself from Yvonne soon after his return to "normal" prison life in September 1915. From this time onward, Rivière was able to turn more simply and less egotistically both to Isabelle and to religion, and he also began to develop a keen interest in the new literary and political projects that would engage his full attention after the war.

Combat and Early Days in Captivity

Rivière's burgeoning sense of religious commitment stands out even in the introductory part of his notebook entitled specifically *Carnet de Guerre,* which treats roughly the first month of his military experience. After the boredom of the first few weeks in training camp, Rivière actually welcomed the move to the front in the region around Verdun on 23 August 1914, and he eagerly anticipated the excitement of combat. His company, aided by other French units in the area, was trying to push back the steadily advancing German troops that were quickly overrunning the villages in the region. On 24 August they set up camp at

the edge of a heavily forested area near the already half-destroyed
village of Eton, waiting for the opportunity to join in the fray.

Somewhat like a schoolboy taking part in a real football game
for the first time, Rivière was at first exhilarated at the thought
of the danger around him; the war was not yet a reality, only a
product of his imagination. His buoyancy and enthusiasm, however, were shortlived. As the battle in the surrounding forest
grew more intense and the possibility for a French victory in the
encounter more remote, his energetic fascination was quickly
transformed into apprehension and fear. The only thing that
helped Rivière keep a basic sense of equilibrium throughout the
trying evening and the nerve-racking night that followed was his
confidence in Divine Providence. As he expressed it, "My confidence in God remained complete, absolute, unshaken" (C, 29).

At nightfall Rivière and his men were still on guard near the
edge of the forest where their captain had positioned them earlier.
After the fighting that had taken place during the day, they
found themselves completely surrounded by Germans, and they
had no choice but to remain where they were, waiting for some
break in the circle of German soldiers to be able to rejoin the
other French units farther away. Rivière felt both frustrated about
their inaction and, as sergeant, deeply responsible for his men.
He sought to remedy the situation by finding an escape route
through the forest. Several times during the night he left the
others, groping his way through the trees in a desperate attempt
to discover a way out of their dilemma, but his well-intentioned
efforts were to no avail. By morning he and his men were prisoners
of the Germans, who had completely overrun the forest during
the night. Rivière's initial reaction to his capture was one of
humiliation and stunned resignation. He was at this point suffering from the shock of the whole episode, not yet fully com-
prehending what had happened to him and moving mechanically
when commanded to do so by the guards. After marching in long
columns past occupied villages to a point near the German border,
the French prisoners were then herded into a train for the long
trip across Germany to their destination, the prisoner-of-war

camp at Koenigsbrück in Saxony, where they arrived on 29 August and where Rivière was to spend nearly three years of his life.

Once Rivière was settled in the routine of camp activities, he turned his attention to his private notebooks, which express the full extent of his anguish and shame about the events leading up to his capture and indicate the already high degree of his religious commitment. It could be said that the stylistic condensation which he had noted as being so important in *Le Sacre du printemps* or in the final version of Rimbaud's *Illuminations* a few months earlier now dominated his own personal outlook. Totally cut off from the companionship and the intellectual stimulation of those whose love and friendship he valued most, Rivière, too, began concentrating on essentials, which in the early days of his captivity consisted, to a large extent, of confessing his humiliation and guilt about what had recently happened at the front. He had wanted to lead his men out of their dilemma and thereby live up to the mental picture of courage and self-importance he had created in his imagination. His failure and his shame were immediate and complete. Since he was captured, he would have no opportunity in the near future to try again to retrieve some of his lost self-respect.

Yet strangely enough, the very depth of Rivière's humiliation worked for him in two different but equally important ways. On the one hand, it helped satisfy his persistent need for suffering, which he considered to be an indication of personal sensitivity. On the other hand, it forced him to confront the full extent of his egoism. He approached religion in the early days of his captivity through the contrition expressed in a prayer from the Mass, the "Confiteor," and strove above all to deepen his appreciation for the dogmas and the rituals of the Church. Religious commitment at this point was, understandably, a kind of compensation for his isolation and a source of stability in a painfully confusing situation.

Along with being tormented by the events surrounding his capture, Rivière was also deeply troubled by what he perceived as his failure with his best friend, Henri. On 4 November 1914, Rivière received a letter from Isabelle which informed him that

Fournier had dissappeared during a battle near Verdun on 22 September. Rivière was overwhelmed by the news and agonized over the way he had treated Fournier during the previous year as well as over his friend's fate on the battlefield. Rivière felt that he had been cold, distant, and reticent with Fournier; he had not offered his friend the support and companionship he needed at what was an important turning point in Fournier's life. During that year Fournier's novel *Le Grand Meaulnes,* which, among other things, depicted his anguish over an impossible love situation, had finally appeared in print. In this same period, Fournier had also corresponded with the young woman who had inspired the character Yvonne de Galais in the novel and realized that this chapter of his life was closed forever. He had likewise embarked on a totally different kind of relationship with a very well known actress, Madame Simone, whom both Rivière and his wife, Isabelle, disapproved of intensely, and he blamed himself for letting this happen. As he indicated in his notebook, "I have my own share in this unfortunate situation . . . I did not sustain him enough" (*C,* 86). Rivière felt that, because of his own selfishness, he had refused Fournier the support that could have kept him from falling into what Rivière saw as a very distressing situation.

Rivière's assessment of the problem, however, was, according to Isabelle's judgment, not very accurate. In the footnotes to Rivière's war notebooks, she carefully points out that he did not mistreat his friend and could in no way be considered responsible for any unhappiness Fournier may have experienced. Yet even though his guilt was unfounded, Rivière still suffered deeply over what he perceived as his neglect of his friend and the image of the horror Fournier had encountered on the battlefield. The two young men had gone through adolescence and entered adulthood together. They had shared their most intimate fears, their most passionate ambitions, and their most inspiring dreams. Alone, completely powerless, and already sensitized by the humiliation of his capture, it is not surprising that Rivière, in this instance, too, concentrated on what he believed to be his insufficiencies, which seemed even more glaring to him because of the irremediability of his loss.

The Writing of *Aimée*

With the isolation and humiliation of the war, religious contemplation became Rivière's mainstay, and he quickly developed an intimate, one-to-one relationship with God. The war was a catalyst which unleashed his spiritual energy and enabled him to understand more clearly than ever before the kind of personal bond that could develop between an individual and his creator. He later said that "Every conversion is a question of an encounter,"[5] and with the onset of the war he finally experienced the kind of direct, painful confrontation with God that profoundly changed his attitude toward religion. As legitimate and sincere as this new intimacy was, however, it was also extremely ambivalent because of its association with the kind of experience Rivière had, on certain occasions, shared with Yvonne and which seemed all the more important to him because of his current isolation. Rivière himself admitted in November 1914 that "I found with God the intimacy that corresponded to that which I had found with her [Yvonne] . . ." (*C,* 94). During the first year of captivity he was torn, on the one hand, between religion and Yvonne and, on the other, between Isabelle and Yvonne. His love for Isabelle coexisted and vied with his passion for Yvonne, which in turn somewhat corresponded to and coexisted with his new religious fervor. In a sense, he wanted to preserve all three of these relationships. As Rivière put it at one point, "Since my youth I felt the need for two women at the same time, the capacity in me to love them simultaneously" (*C,* 104). He wished to enjoy both the tranquillity and the normalcy he associated with Isabelle along with the intellectual excitement inspired by Yvonne and, at the same time, continue to make progress spiritually. He sought to maintain three different, simultaneous relationships of equal magnitude and, in a way, devote himself completely to each one of them.

Most of the time, however, the essential ambivalence of Rivière's sentiments is painfully obvious. Examining the notebook entries from November 1914 through the following summer, we can easily discern the degree of Rivière's confusion and the depth of his struggle between the kind of love represented by the two

women in his life in relation to his spiritual awareness. His love
for Isabelle is depicted in terms of physical well-being, whereas
his love for Yvonne is described in terms of illness and torment.
With Isabelle he has a rapport that is "living and profound" (*C,*
95), while his relationship with Yvonne is "immense and sterile"
(*C,* 95). Despite his well-intentioned attempts to do so, he could
neither balance these two relationships satisfactorily nor relinquish his psychological commitment to Yvonne. He was hope-
lessly entangled in a web of conflicting emotions from which he
could not extricate himself.

During the first dismal winter at Koenigsbrück, possibly near
the particularly sensitive time in February that marked the an-
niversary of what he called his psychological captivity, Rivière
began working on his novel *Aimée.*[6] Although he revised the
manuscript extensively even to the point of rewriting many sections, *Aimée,* as it was finally published in 1922, treats precisely
the psychological crisis which he experienced during the war
years.[7] No sooner had Rivière begun this project than he noted
that "All of my remaining strength [is] drained by my work
. . . it is this which sustains me, but it is also this which eats
away at me. . . . Again . . . the torture of writing" (*C,* 197).
The anguish that had tormented him during the past several
months was transferred to this long-dreamed-of and long-delayed
project. As we have seen earlier, Rivière struggled for many years
to write a novel, and now he found that he had not only the
inspiration, but also the time to concentrate on the task. There
were no publication deadlines to be met, no secretarial duties to
distract him. From the outset, work on *Aimée* was an extremely
beneficial activity for Rivière because it focused his attention
away from his personal suffering and forced him once again to
think about literary problems, such as characterization and plot
development. The work exhausted him, but it did change the
angle from which he considered his psychological situation and
kept him from becoming either more confused or more polarized
in his reactions.

Throughout the spring and early summer of 1915, Rivière
made steady progress with his novel, and he also prepared to

change prison camps. Earlier in the year German military officials had heard rumors that their officers who had been captured in battle by the French were being guarded by blacks in French prison camps. Enraged by what they considered an insult to their racial superiority, the Germans were quick to retaliate by setting up reprisal camps to punish the French for this special humiliation inflicted on the German officers. The reprisal camps, which were far more primitive and located in much more isolated regions than ordinary prisoner-of-war compounds, were designed especially for the intellectual elite of the French prisoners, who were unaccustomed to hard physical labor. Those who were selected for duty in these special camps were to spend each entire day digging up a certain amount of land around the camp as if they were preparing it for planting, and the Germans were careful to assure that the areas assigned would be much too large for even the strongest worker to finish in the time allotted.[8]

When Rivière saw the notice announcing that some of the inmates at Koenigsbrück would soon be leaving for the Hülseberg reprisal camp, 170 kilometers from the Dutch border, he quickly volunteered to go. His offer was inspired not so much by magnanimity, however, as by his decision to organize an escape attempt. Rivière believed that it was his duty to try to escape from a frustrating situation in which he was of no use to his country. He wanted at least to try to get back into combat. The season of the year and the proximity of the reprisal camp to the border were in his favor. Consequently he and a companion, Pasquier, called Fritz, worked out the details of their project and gradually collected the supplies and civilian clothes which would be so crucial to the success of their effort.

After several postponements in the departure schedule, the prisoners finally left Koenigsbrück and arrived at Hülseberg on 20 July 1915. By the end of the month, Rivière and Pasquier were ready, and on 2 August the two men managed to slip unnoticed out of the work column into the dense underbrush surrounding the work site where they had hidden their provisions and started on their journey. For several days all seemed to be going well, but on the fourth day the whole project backfired.

While passing through a village, they were questioned by a group of local citizens and were quickly recognized not only as foreigners, but as escaped prisoners. They were taken back to Hülseberg, where they were interrogated and then sentenced to thirty-five days in solitary confinement in such primitive conditions that the rest of the camp seemed almost luxurious by comparison. Through the ingeniousness of their fellow prisoners, however, Rivière and Pasquier received some extra provisions, which sustained them during their days of imposed fast.

With the help of a special friend, Rivière even managed to get meager writing materials and immediately set to work completing the draft of the last and, he felt, most crucial chapter of his novel, in which he would deal with the final stages of his protagonist's separation from Aimée and his return to his wife, Marthe. Rivière put particular care into this chapter because it described the kind of change he himself was undergoing at that time and because he wished to emphasize the importance of Marthe, who had waited patiently and calmly in the background throughout the whole series of experiences depicted in the earlier chapters. As Rivière was diligently working on the manuscript one morning in his cell, however, the guards burst in unexpectedly and wrenched the papers away from him before he realized what was happening, adding one more humiliation to those they had already inflicted on him. When Rivière appeared before the officer in charge later that day, the lieutenant ridiculed Rivière's text— "these imbecilities" (*C,* 257), as he called them—but he refused to give the papers back to the prisoner. The loss of these precious pages over which he had agonized for so many days was, to Rivière, irrevocable. He had written the chapter in a state of inspired tension and never again found the same kind of momentum that had inspired his work on the last chapter during his days in solitary confinement.

As soon as he had completed his sentence, Rivière was transferred on 9 September 1915 back to Koenigsbrück, which was too far from any free border to permit another escape attempt. At first he wondered if he would ever return to his notebooks. "What I would like to inscribe there is so vast, so complex that

I don't know how to seize it" (*C,* 257). But his hesitation was only momentary. Almost immediately Rivière began describing what he termed "the slow revolution in my heart" (*C,* 262), his renewed commitment to Isabelle and his growing indifference to Yvonne. "With the joy that I felt in receiving this letter from Isabelle, I felt that the other *thing* was finished, conquered, killed . . ." (*C,* 280). Although part of Rivière still clung to the remnants of a memory that obsessed him and although he would continue to defend Yvonne in the face of criticism from others,[9] he had made his choice and easily followed through with his decision. Over the next two years of his captivity his references to Yvonne would become fewer and fewer, and the nature of his comments more explicitly negative. He had come to realize the limitations of his relationship with her and knew that the intellectual pleasure he had enjoyed in her company would no longer tempt him.

Although Rivière's move away from Yvonne in the months immediately following his escape attempt was definite and decisive, his depiction of the whole drawn-out experience, including the final stages of the crisis, in his novel is not nearly so clear. All of the ambivalence and confusion which surrounded the situation filtered into the fictional treatment of the dilemma. To be exact, *Aimée* is not really a novel at all, but rather a monologue or a thinly veiled autobiographical portrait of a still adolescent aspect of Rivière's mentality, and the work bears no resemblance at all to the dynamic, all-encompassing creation whose characteristics Rivière had described so passionately and so lucidly in "Le Roman d'aventure." As he had regretfully noted several years before, he lacked the kind of concrete imagination which is so indispensable to a novelist. His style is overwhelmingly academic, his dialogues are stilted, and his character depiction is excessively cerebral. There is no movement or sense of adventure in *Aimée* because even on a strictly psychological level nothing significant ever really happens. The entire work is interiorized; no conflict with exterior reality ever occurs. The subtle emotional transformations which the protagonist does experience take place in such a distilled atmosphere that they lose much of their authenticity.

The book centers around the persistent, though painfully in-
decisive efforts of a young married man who, though he loves his
wife, seeks the affections of another young woman in order to
make his life more exciting. The work opens with François, the
principal male character, describing his attitude toward the fe-
male sex. He reacts to women as one might to a finely chiseled
sculpture or a delicate Symbolist poem which exist solely for the
pleasure and agitation they can arouse in sensitive souls. When,
as a young man, he comes to Paris to seek his fortune, François's
gaze dreamily follows the enticing but ethereal forms he sees all
around him in the streets and gardens. A year after his arrival
in Paris, he meets a naive, innocent, unpretentious young teacher
named Marthe to whom he is drawn because of her physical
fragility and whom he quickly grows to love for her tenderness
and quiet stability. For her part, Marthe returns François's affection with complete openness. Both the period of their en-
gagement and the early months of their marriage are a time of
"infinite peace."[10] It is, however, the very tranquillity of their
relationship which soon begins to irritate François. He wants to
suffer in love and consequently sets out to find this kind of
experience elsewhere, leaving Marthe to wait patiently for his
return.

Through the intervention of his more worldly, experienced
friend Georges Bourguignon, François soon meets Georges's fi-
ancée, Aimée Laval, whom Georges had earlier described in rather
ambiguous terms, stressing the intensity of her personality and
the independence of her spirit. From the moment of their first
brief conversation together, François is struck by the openness,
the directness, and the simplicity of Aimée's manner. As he learns
more of her from Georges, who attends more and more social
functions alone, hears the story of Aimée's unfortunate childhood,
and sees Aimée herself at times outwardly anxious and restless,
François begins to pity her, hoping in this way to win her affection
and confidence. In this area, though, François is sorely disap-
pointed, for pity is the last sentiment that Aimée wishes to inspire
or to which she can respond, and the more frustrated François
becomes in his efforts to get her to succumb to his pity, the more

obsessive his attraction to her becomes. When Georges nonchalantly announces one day that Aimée will soon leave Paris for a rest in the country, François realizes with ecstatic satisfaction that he loves her—thoroughly enjoying the pain he is experiencing. In fact, as François himself stresses, "The more I suffered the more sure I was."[11] And from this time on, his life becomes a series of increasingly intense torments caused by Aimée's indifference to his passion.

The kind of bizarre relationship that gradually develops between François and Aimée is somewhat difficult to define because of ambiguities in the text itself. It is, in our opinion, unclear as to exactly how much of Aimée's attitude toward François is direct friendship, how much intellectual teasing, and how much egotistical self-indulgence. On the one hand, she relies on François (who is nearly always there) both for companionship and as an escort when Georges is socializing elsewhere. Aimée told François at their first meeting that she considered him her friend, and she treats him quite openly and without subterfuge. On the other hand, we should stress that in some of the scenes where Aimée and François engage in their favorite pastime—penetrating character examination—she appears cold and merciless. From the first time Georges mentions Aimée to François, the term "hardness" is frequently used to refer to her glances, her laugh, or the tone of her voice, and, at times, she does seem to be taking advantage of François's pathetic vulnerability for her own pleasure. She delights in his interrogations about who she really is and in his revelations about her cruelty. If Aimée is at times cold and totally self-centered, it should also be noted that she is by no means alone in her selfishness. François, too, is guilty of the same kind of egocentricity. Each one is, to a great extent, independently pursuing an adventure in self-awareness and self-satisfaction at the other's expense. And for all of her hardness and often-mentioned intellectual solitude, Aimée seems to us in the long run much more honest, more vital, and more interested in a truly reciprocal relationship than François, who cannot progress beyond the stage of feeling pity for her and himself and establish a bond on more positive grounds.

Despite her outbursts of cruelty, Aimée appears to us not cold, but rather direct and open. Like Rivière himself during the war, Aimée refuses the condescending attitude of pity as the basis for a viable relationship.[12] She definitely is unfair to François by allowing him to visit so frequently, by requesting him to accompany her on various outings, and by using his attention to develop greater self-understanding. But she does not deceive him or ever lead him to think that she feels anything more than concern and affection for him. François, for his part, fully recognizes this, but he cannot be satisfied with friendship. François wants much more from Aimée, and, at various points in his musings, he blames his lack of success with her on his sexual timidity. The real source of conflict between them, however, stems precisely from the fact that François keeps trying to extort something from Aimée which she cannot give him. And Aimée's inability to feel anything *more* than friendship for François comes not from her coldness and sterility, but rather from the exclusiveness of her attachment to Georges. Aimée is completely committed to her husband and has been from the moment she met him. As she explains to François during one of their last conversations, "Until that time I had been touched, of course, by more than one countenance . . . but from the first moment I felt that I had to go to him; it hit me squarely in the face. Legally or not—it made no difference to me—I had to be his wife. If he hadn't wanted to marry me, I would certainly have become his mistress."[13] These are not, in our opinion, the kind of remarks that would be made by a heartless person incapable of profound feelings for others.

Aimée both greatly loves her husband and values the friendship François has offered her. As she emphasizes once again a bit further on in this same conversation, "You are my only true friend. . . ."[14] She has been thoughtless, self-centered, and at times mysteriously cruel. Yet she also truly regrets having added to François's suffering through her own egocentricity[15] and is very happy when, at length, he can understand the kind of affection she has felt all along for him. François finally is able to admit to himself, "She appreciates you, she feels tenderness for you . . . she is grateful. . . . She doesn't love you and she'll never love you."[16] But it is also important to note that François does not give Aimée up out of nobleness, magnanimity, or newly discovered spiritual insight. Nor does he come to see her as a monster, as has so often been indicated. Rather, through Aimée's own explanations, he learns to face the *total* futility of his entire pursuit.

When the two finally part company outside the country inn where Aimée has gone to rest, François pauses for a long moment during which he contemplates suicide, as he had done once before earlier in the work. But his attention is diverted by "the image of Marthe,"[17] radiant with tenderness, which he fathoms coming forth from the shadows to welcome him back. The book ends with this scene of implied reconciliation, which is confused because the text itself never clarifies whether Marthe is actually there or whether François imagines the whole meeting as he had imagined his relationship with Aimée.

Marthe has been totally in the shadows from the very early pages of the book, and the portrait presented of her is sketchy and sadly incomplete. From François's own description of Marthe in the first chapter, she would seem to have little in common with the awesome, captivating Aimée, whose presence dominates the work. And yet, despite the differences between them, the two women share many of the same positive qualities. Both Marthe and Aimée are described as direct, simple, and unpretentious. Both of them have suffered, but they refuse to be overwhelmed by their sufferings. Each of the two women is also depicted as having a concern for order, and each possesses a kind of discipline, inner direction, and sense of personal identity which the adolescent male characters lack completely. Although by no means parallel, it is the two women who give the book depth, psychological complexity, and a certain sense of mystery. Were it not for the personal equilibrium of Marthe and the dynamism of Aimée, the work would be unbearable. Their presence redeems it somewhat and saves it from deteriorating into a totally abstract dissertation.

Spiritual Affirmation

Although generally unsuccessful as a work of narrative fiction, *Aimée* reveals the subtlety of Rivière's analytical powers and indirectly indicates the depth of his admiration for and confidence in the two women characters, for only they are in any way depicted positively. Georges is a frivolous social butterfly, and François vacillates between self-admiration and self-pity. Rivière's ambivalence about his own feelings for Aimée and Marthe and his persistent uncertainty concerning his self-image stand out even in the much-reworked published form of his wartime novel. The eminent Catholic critic Charles Du Bos, in his sensitive review of *Aimée* for the *NRF,* refers to François's experience as an ardent pursuit of the absolute.[18] Although we could legitimately argue about the appropriateness of this epithet as applied to the novel, it does accurately describe Rivière's own personal evolution in the months after he completed the draft of *Aimée* in the autumn of 1915.

Rivière felt personally touched by the hand of Divine Providence in a totally unexpected way, first through the humiliation of his captivity and then through the agony of his time in solitary confinement. He began to feel the unique impact of Christian dogmas on his own life. They were no longer abstractions but concrete realities which became an integral part of his own experience. There were no more doubts and no more torturing questions to retard his progress further. With the anguish of his relationship with Yvonne behind him and his renewed dedication to Isabelle growing continually, Rivière entered into his most intense period of spiritual jubilation. There were still days when he had to struggle violently with feelings of vanity and moments of despondency when he felt completely empty and exhausted. But, for the most part, Rivière's comments on religion in his notebooks from the autumn of 1915 onward become much less self-conscious and guilt-ridden. They express instead his passionate commitment to God, his sincere desire to serve others, and his gratitude for his growing sense of equilibrium. The religious quotations scattered throughout Rivière's notebooks but concentrated in the sections following his return to Koenigsbrück clearly indicate the nature of his spiritual growth. Quotations from St. Theresa of Avila's autobiography, from St. Francis de Sales's *Imitation of Christ* and from St. Augustine's *Confessions* appear most frequently; by comparing the quotations with Rivière's comments about them, we can clearly discern the new, uplifting tone and the greater depth of his conviction.

Rivière's faith became simultaneously more personal and more extroverted. On the one hand, he notes the mystical quality of certain situations when "I was truly in a great religious trance . . ." (*C,* 274). More and more frequently he experienced moments of communion with God when all the pieces of the puzzle over which he had struggled for so long in his search for truth fell easily into place. On the other hand, Rivière's faith could not exist in a vacuum. He needed activities which would, in a sense, authenticate his new fervor. After a period of concentrated introspection, he was once again ready to confront the world around him.

As Rivière's own religious commitment developed, he wished to announce his certitude to others and encourage them to consider the impact Christianity could have on their own lives. Consequently he organized a series of lectures to discuss informally the importance of Catholicism in twentieth-century Europe. Rivière made only sparse, indirect references to this project in his notebooks (see, for example, the entries for 27 November 1915 and 31 December 1915), and it is only through Isabelle's explanatory notes that the situation becomes clear. In order to make the time spent as a prisoner more profitable, Rivière suggested to a small group of fellow inmates that each one of them prepare an informal talk on a subject which interested him to present to the rest of the group. After Rivière's death in 1925, Isabelle assembled the notes for Rivière's own lectures and published them under the title of *A la Trace de Dieu,* along with short excerpts from the notebooks themselves. The thrust of spiritual enthusiasm and self-assurance which animates the entries in Rivière's war journal from late 1915 on likewise inspires the notes that make up *A la Trace de Dieu.* Although rough and unpolished, they are nevertheless important for the further light they shed on the nature of Rivière's spiritual commitment and for the way in which they reveal his desire to synthesize religious and social concerns.

The text of *A la Trace de Dieu* is divided into seven chapters, each of which examines a specific religious issue. In each section of his discussion, Rivière emphasizes the necessity for total personal commitment to Catholicism, and he also extols the broadness and the expansiveness of the dogmas which form the basis of its theological structure. Just as he had stressed in one of his prewar letters to Gide that Catholicism was vast enough to accommodate all human characteristics (see Chapter 3, section II), so too does Rivière again praise the broad, all-inclusive quality of this religion, which does not recoil from any absurdity, even the horrors of war. It encompasses and responds to all aspects of the human condition. There is, however, one important difference between Rivière's prewar comments on the vastness of Catholicism and statements in *A la Trace de Dieu*—a difference which reveals one of his new areas of interest. In his letter to Gide, Rivière was speaking on a strictly private, individual level, whereas in *A la Trace de Dieu* are included historical, social, and political phenomena as well. As his understanding and appreciation of Catholicism broadened, so also did his own field of concern; when his private anguish diminished, he was able to turn his attention toward other things and examine the complex sociopolitical problems confronting not only France, but all of Europe.

Two entire chapters of Rivière's lecture notes are devoted to specifically social issues. One deals with the relationship between the Church and social concerns in general, while the other treats Catholicism's attitude toward war. Both of these discussions are in turn directly related to the detailed social and political reflections in Rivière's war notebooks, which begin in the fall of 1916 and continue throughout the remaining months of his captivity. One of the earliest entries where Rivière's new political interest comes to the fore is dated 10 December 1916: "This outbreak of rage, this tempest of good will during Mass. Not really religious. Political rather. The tremendous need to serve my country. . . . I saw that after the war I could not go back to the disinterested and quite speculative attitude which I had before" (*C,* 370). No longer could he sit back in his study and devote himself exclusively to literary pursuits. As he emphasized, "I want to serve; I want to be good for something" (*C,* 371). No longer troubled by painful memories or religious doubts, he was eager to get out and do something concrete for the benefit of humanity. And, in our opinion, it is particularly important that this kind of illumination occurred to him during Mass. Similar to the way in which the war triggered Rivière's personal conversion, now it is his spiritual confidence which acts as a springboard to social involvement. His religious exaltation began to renew his psychological energy so that he could focus his attention on the work to be done after the war.

Rivière believed that he had acquired the psychological equilibrium and the maturity to be of service to humanity. One of his fellow prisoners declared that "There is a time to absorb and a time to expound . . . he determined around age 30 the appearance of this new need which completely changes the meaning of one's life . . ." (*C,* 416). Rivière felt that this was precisely the kind of transformation he was undergoing at this time. There were urgent problems that had to be dealt with if Europe was to recover from the devastation of the war, and, despite his mental fatigue, Rivière was eager to participate in the rebuilding process.

The Portraits of *L'Allemand* and *Le Français*

Before Rivière could give his full attention to genuine reconstruction, however, he had to unleash the pent-up frustration and anger which his years in captivity inspired; he did so when he wrote *L'Allemand*. Unable to confront the enemy on the battlefield, Rivière entered into direct mental combat with the German temperament in this work. In the preface to the first edition he openly insists that "I am yielding here, knowing it full well, to the fury of my spirit . . . ,"[19] and it is extremely important to bear this in mind when dealing with this particular book. It is unlike anything Rivière had ever written before or would write again because of its degree of invective and the totality of its condemnation. The writing of *L'Allemand,* similar to that of

Aimée, represented a kind of spiritual exorcism which he had to undergo before the psychological wounds he had suffered could even begin to heal.

Rivière's arguments are divided into two principal sections which are supposed to present the Germans from two different points of view. In the first part of his discussion entitled "D'Après Nature," he pinpoints the main characteristics of the German temperament based on the evidence he personally accumulated while at Koenigsbrück. The German character is, first of all, completely lacking in any fundamental preferences or meditative ability. The German "has at first neither desires nor dreams; neither love nor hatred . . . ," and because of this void at the very center of his being, he reacts mechanically to situations, blindly carrying out orders without ever considering their significance or the effect they might have on others. Animated by the sheer force of will power which takes the place of all other forms of psychological sensitivity or intellectual refinement, the German temperament continually seeks new projects to organize and new domains to conquer in order to extend the sphere of its physical influence as far as possible in all directions.

In the second section of his discussion, Rivière reiterates in slightly different terms the main points presented in the first part of his description; his approach to the whole situation in this part is more indirect and ingenious but, at the same time, more insidious. He summarizes a highly flattering portrait of the German mentality made by a contemporary German philosopher, Paul Natorp, and then proceeds to rip Natorp's arguments to shreds by showing how Natorp's own remarks support the negative interpretation Rivière himself had presented in the first part of his essay. There is a certain element of truth in many of Rivière's comments, but any cultural value that his portrait could have is almost totally negated, in our opinion, by his overwhelming personal prejudice against the Germans. He is influenced, not only by the strong sense of nationalistic antagonism which existed between France and Germany long before the war broke out, but also by the humiliation of his experience as a prisoner. *L'Allemand* stands in sharp contrast to the open-mindedness which

Rivière continually exhibited in his aesthetic articles and to the unpretentiousness of both his *Carnets* and *A la Trace de Dieu*. In his essay on the Germans, Rivière seems to be acting as both judge and jury, convicting an entire nation of crimes against twentieth-century civilization and passing sentence on it. Although the reason *why* Rivière had to write *L'Allemand* is quite understandable, the narrow perspective and the unrestricted generalizations in this work flagrantly conflict with the sense of fairness and the precision which characterize Rivière's thought as a whole.

Rivière's text *Le Français* stands as somewhat of a counterpoint to his hostile description of the Germans. Like *L'Allemand*, this work too consists of a series of reflections which Rivière made during his captivity and which were eventually assembled for publication in 1928. He wrote the work ostensibly to diagnose the general intellectual and psychological problems facing his countrymen during World War I and suggest remedies for them, but Rivière's national prejudice clouds his vision. Just as his negative attitude toward the Germans comes across immediately in *L'Allemand*, so also does Rivière's firm belief in the superiority of the French temperament and its way of perceiving reality stand out in even the opening pages of *Le Français*. Despite his criticisms concerning the potential dangers of the French people's notorious individualism and universal passion for ideas, it is obvious that their virtues and accomplishments far outweigh their faults.

Rivière is convinced of the complete superiority of the French people, of the uniqueness of their attitudes, and of the importance of their national mission, "to indicate the place of great spiritual values, to prevent them from being replaced by other things."[20] Because of his subjectivity and the narrowness of his point of view, *Le Français*, like *L'Allemand*, has only limited value. Through their very insufficiencies, however, these two works attest to the importance of developing a broader, more international outlook that is not so deeply entrenched in stereotyped nationalistic concepts. They manifest the need for the more relative, more modest kind of nationalism which Rivière hinted at in *A la Trace de Dieu* and in his war notebooks and which he was

able to develop in depth for the postwar benefit of both himself
and his country.

The first published article where a broader perspective and a
sense of international tolerance begin to dominate Rivière's vision
is an essay written soon after his release from Koenigsbrück, in
which he explains in detail the reasons why a League of Nations
must be formed. Rivière recognizes that, despite the conflicts
over national differences and specific nationalistic interests, such
an organization is indispensable if Europe is to recover from the
war and prosper again. Men must look beyond the frontiers of
their individual countries, realizing that more than ever before
"The cause of the individual has become that of everyone."[21]
Rivière still stresses the importance of what he sees as national
differences and does not seek to substitute concern for humanity
in general for love of one's country, but, as he insists, the war
"has made us understand, underneath racial differences, the similarity of conditions."[22] The two kinds of commitment should
coexist, forming a synthesis between self-interest and altruism,
and, as Rivière concludes, "The equilibrium which would be
established in this way . . . is the best guarantee to peace which
can be imagined."[23] Rivière would at times despair of ever realizing the project for European reconstruction briefly outlined
in this article, but he never retracted his belief in the need for
pursuing such a dream.[24]

Rivière's analysis of Europe's postwar needs outlined in his
article on the League of Nations contrasts sharply with the portraits presented in *L'Allemand* and *Le Français*. The narrow, nationalistic comments in these latter works are, quite fortunately,
not representative of Rivière's overall political attitude. It is,
rather, the sensitive concern for all European countries and the
acceptance of other points of view that characterize Rivière's political thought as it does his approach to aesthetic issues, and his
activities upon his return to France would bring the extent of
this commitment into full view.

Recuperation and Intellectual
Renewal in Switzerland

Before turning our attention to the postwar years when Rivière would serve as the controversial director of the prestigious *NRF*, we must briefly examine the significance of the little-discussed transitional period he spent in Switzerland. It was during his stay there that Rivière began to recuperate from the war and to lay the groundwork for the renewal and reconstruction projects to be undertaken in France.

In May 1916, the Red Cross completed an agreement with the German government which allowed French prisoners no longer capable of combat duty to spend the remainder of the war in Switzerland with minimum-security restrictions. During that summer, Rivière's family and friends began the task of securing his release from Koenigsbrück. Through the efforts of Isabelle, Jacques Copeau, his close friend from the early *NRF* group, and the help of certain Swiss writers, such as C.-F. Ramuz, Rivière's name was brought to the attention of the authorities as someone who would qualify for a move to Switzerland. Despite his fragile health, Rivière at first violently rejected the idea, saying that it would be cowardly. But with a little persuasion from Isabelle, he soon agreed that this would be the most beneficial course both for him personally and for his commitment to his country. It took nearly a year to work through the endless red tape, during which time Rivière became more and more impatient with camp life and eager about the possibility of directing the *NRF*, which Gallimard first hinted at in early 1917. With the arrangements completed, Rivière finally arrived in the town of Engelburg, Switzerland, on 14 June 1917, and Isabelle and their little daughter Jacqueline joined him there the following month.

Although weak, exhausted, and somewhat overwhelmed by the return to something approximating civilian life, Rivière began to work almost immediately. The various personal and professional documents published under the title *Jacques Rivière et ses amitiés suisses* provide us with important details concerning Rivière's activities during this period; they reveal the growth of his reputation as a critic in Switzerland and indicate the way in which he paved the way for the extensive collaboration and intellectual exchange that would take place between the rising young group of Swiss critics and the *NRF* when the review resumed publication in 1919.

Soon after his arrival in Engelburg, Rivière received a visit from his old friend Jacques Copeau, but despite the sincere effort on both their parts, the two men were never able to recapture the intimacy they had shared before the war. They had both changed too much. As Rivière wrote to Copeau nearly two years after this reunion, " 'No, we never really met or found one another again.' "25 But despite their feeling of personal estrangement, they spent many fruitful hours conversing about literary issues and, as Rivière stressed in a letter to one of his aunts, "the resumption of the review."26 Soon after Copeau left, Gide arrived, bringing what Rivière described as "other ideas, other subjects for reflection, once again launching me in new directions."27 Rivière profited greatly from these conversations, for it had been many years since he had been able to discuss what was still one of his most passionate interests with individuals whose literary insights he respected and admired. As he noted a little further on in the same letter, "It did me a lot of good because I need this kind of mental activity in order to feel myself living."28 Despite occasional attacks of psychological inertia, Rivière was gradually recovering some of the intellectual energy and mental suppleness which he felt he had lost during the years of his captivity.

During the early days of his stay in Engelburg, Rivière also began to correspond with various Swiss authors, such as Ramuz, who had helped in his release effort, and with those writers associated with the series called *Les Cahiers vaudois,* published in the French canton of Vaud. They suggested that Rivière try to procure a transfer to French Switzerland so that he could be nearer to them and to his homeland, and they also asked Rivière to collaborate on some new literary projects. At first Rivière resisted the idea of leaving Engelburg. He was physically tired, and he had already developed a sense of calm security about the city.

But in December when he received government authorization, he finally decided to move to Geneva and spent the remaining months of his stay in Switzerland in this city.

Once in Geneva, Rivière began again to attend the theater and other literary gatherings, he took a substitute teaching post, and, most importantly, he embarked on a series of informal lectures intitled "La Jeune Littérature française avant 1914." This series was actually the first of several that Rivière would give in Switzerland over the next few years. He would repeat for Swiss audiences in Geneva and Lausanne his lecture series on Proust in March 1923. And in December of the following year, he would debate the highly contested issue of moralism in literature with Ramon Fernandez in both of these Swiss cities.

The talks on prewar French literature, which Rivière started to give in February 1918, marked the official beginning of an intellectual relationship with the Swiss literary public that would continue to grow until the time of Rivière's death. Struck by the precision of his critical remarks and his personal charm, the public immediately felt a new dimension of understanding and appreciation opening before them. The articles by various Swiss critics discussing Rivière's lecture series, which were written and published at the time he gave his talks and later included in *Jacques Rivière et ses amitiés suisses,* are, as far as we can discern, the first formal evaluations of Rivière's literary convictions, and they suggest the kind of literary examination of conscience he was undertaking at the time. Impressed with Rivière's unpretentious self-confidence, his psychological subtlety, and his intellectual acuity, they also detected a note of hesitation in some of his remarks, as if he were rethinking his own position during the talks themselves. As Alexis François noted in his review of one of Rivière's lectures, the *NRF* temple of aesthetic purity in which the best French authors were ensconced before the war was perhaps too aloof, and "Perhaps M. Jacques Rivière himself does not see it [the temple] in quite the same way as before."[29] And in reply to François's comments, Rivière himself openly acknowledged, "You guessed well that I no longer see the works about which I'm talking at this moment in the same light as before the war and that all my reflections are recapitulatory. The future is wide-open. But before launching into it, it is not a bad idea to recapture consciousness of one's past a last time."[30] Rivière was fully aware of the need to take one last, passionate look back and summarize past convictions and preferences before confronting the future, and the lectures in Switzerland provided him with the perfect opportunity to do so.

Although his attitude toward specific authors and, as we shall see, his conception of the *NRF* changed, Rivière would by no means abandon his past concerns. In fact the sense of eager expectation that Rivière expressed in his letter to François closely resembles the reaction which, several years before, he had felt a true adventure novel would inspire—the emotion "of waiting for something, of not yet knowing everything . . . of being brought as near as possible to the threshold of what does not yet exist" (*NE,* 277). In this prewar essay he had applied Descartes's rigorous philosophical lucidity to literary problems. He had spoken out against the vague confusion of Romanticism, the subjectivism of the Symbolist aesthetic, and emphasized the need for clarity, precision, and careful distinction of ideas explaining that "We want [an author] to bring out a thousand, separate, well-formed ideas. Cards on the table: I want to see everything" (*NE,* 264). Rivière wanted to understand everything possible about a particular incident or character in a novel, unhampered by any exterior prohibitions or directives. As the entries in his war notebooks clearly indicate, during the years of his captivity Rivière reread and reflected extensively on the seventeenth-century Classical writers whose lucidity and psychological refinement he had admired so greatly even before the war. Now, after his return to civilian life, he would seek more energetically than ever before to integrate the intellectual and emotional precision which characterized the French Classical tradition with the bursting dynamism of the postwar era in order to create a flexible but firm base for literary, spiritual, and political rebirth.

When Rivière left Switzerland to return to France in the summer of 1918, he was anxious to begin the task for which he had so diligently prepared throughout much of his stay in Switzerland.

As critic Paul Beaulieu comments concerning this final period of Rivière's career as director of the *NRF*, "Under the influence of an interior force which only needed the opportunity to manifest itself. . . he accepted this weighty responsibility and took firmly in hand not only the direction but the orientation of the review."[31] Animated by a growing sense of authority and a clarity of vision, Rivière set out on the adventure of literary and political reconstruction.

Chapter Six

Dedication to Tolerance and Understanding: Rivière's Mature Years with the *NRF*

Rivière's Assertiveness as Director

The first postwar issue of the *NRF* came out in June 1919, introduced by Rivière's controversial manifesto, which boldly defined the nature and the scope of the review's interests and established the strength of his position as head of the undertaking. In contrast to the prewar *NRF* which had been organized and run by a group, the new *NRF* was in the firm control of the director. The actual choice of Rivière for this post was the subject of complicated negotiations on the part of the review's founders. As early as 1916, while Rivière was still a prisoner of war, Jean Schlumberger had written to him concerning his aspirations for the *NRF* after the war and the important role which both he and Gide hoped that Rivière would play in the new organization. Rivière quickly replied with an enthusiastic statement describing, as he put it, how "I have worked out an entire new program in my head."[1] Gide also wrote encouragingly to Rivière stressing that "The future of the *NRF* rests on your shoulders . . . it is your generation and you that the journal must count on for its propelling force."[2] Rivière was eager to accept the challenge which Gide put to him and to his generation and began immediately to work out a general editorial policy which would enable the *NRF* "to see far, deep, and true; I would like it to continue being as free of a priori ideas and attempt solely to comprehend what is taking place, to explain things as they are, never to sacrifice immediate national interest for the higher concern of the country, which above all is to understand."[3]

The original *NRF* organizers unanimously agreed that Rivière's talents were of vital importance if the review were to flourish again after the war. But when it came to officially naming him the director, there was a considerable amount of dissension among the founders. Although he had not stated anything openly, Gide wished to take on the task himself. As Jean Schlumberger notes in his reflections on the postwar history of the *NRF*, "Without saying it too openly, Gide had intended to assume the direction [of the review] himself."[4] As late as February 1919, Gide still thought that he would be the director, but soon thereafter he was forced to abandon the idea. When the influential Claudel heard that it was Gide, arch immoralist in his eyes, who was going to control the *NRF*, he reacted violently; Claudel threatened never again to contribute anything to the *NRF* if Gide did take over the directorship. Anxious to avoid this catastrophe and, at the same time, to give Gide the free time he needed to pursue his creative projects, Schlumberger noted that "We thought it wiser to give the title to Rivière."[5]

Rivière, for his part, fully comprehended the complexity of the problems surrounding the choice of a director. He understood the organizers' hesitation caused by his youth and by his limited editorial experience as a junior member of the prewar *NRF* team. He also knew that his conviction that the review should be firmly controlled by an individual would trigger even more controversy among the founders. As he confided to Isabelle in November 1918, "I am almost asking them for a kind of abdication into my hands. Will they wish to allow themselves to be dethroned like common German princes?"[6] He did not want to usurp power for himself or act discourteously toward Gide and the original editorial committee, but he had well-thought-out ideas about how the review should be run and made it clear that if asked to head the *NRF* his authority would have to equal his title. When the official offer did come, Rivière accepted it enthusiastically, determined to devote the best of himself to the effort. As he would soon find, however, he would have to defend his position in the face of criticism from a number of different sources.

In his manifesto heading the first postwar issue, Rivière outlined the task ahead of the *NRF* and set the tone for all of his own future contributions to the review. The prewar *NRF* had been conceived as a teamwork project and founded on the principles of open-mindedness and aesthetic autonomy. It had appealed to men's noblest aspirations and had attempted to create "a rigorously pure atmosphere, which would foster the blooming of completely open works" (*NE,* 285). Inspired by the same concern for complete artistic liberty which had animated the review's founders, Rivière reiterated the supreme importance of this conviction as the guiding spirit behind the new publication— "We wish once again to create an impartial journal" (*NE,* 285). He reasserted his unaltered belief in the value of artistic creation as such. Despite the fact that the war had shaken the very foundation of Western culture, Rivière felt, perhaps too idealistically, "that literature is literature, that art is art" (*NE,* 285). In contrast to the Dadaists who insisted that aesthetic endeavors were as corrupt as every other aspect of Western civilization and should be destroyed, Rivière saw this realm of human activity as the one that had been preserved from the immediate destruction of the war itself and, as such, offered hope for the future. He was perhaps naive and extreme in his statements concerning the unchanging nature of aesthetic activity, but his extremism was dictated by what he understood as the urgency of the present situation—the need to preserve what was worthwhile from the past and begin rebuilding immediately.

In his lead article, Rivière also reaffirmed that criteria for determining the significance of a particular work of art had to come from the way in which the various aspects within the work itself coordinated to form a whole rather than from any exterior directives. It was completely wrong, Rivière felt, to judge artistic creations according to the dictates of moral, social, or political concerns. For more than four years France's creative resources had been drained by the tension of the war which had forced the country to concentrate on specific, nationalistic concerns. However necessary such direction and restraint may have been during the war years, it was now time to free the imagination and, as Rivière put it, cultivate "a certain gratuitousness" (*NE,* 286) or sense of independence in all areas of artistic endeavor, so that the promise of authentic creativity could once again be realized. And he expressed his sincere hope that the *NRF* would be "the speculative organ" (*NE,* 288) that France so seriously needed at the time in order to re-establish a sense of artistic equilibrium. He had great expectations that the *NRF* would become an intellectual crossroads of truly international dimensions where many different kinds of creators could come together to share their efforts with others and initiate provocative critical exchanges.

It should be noted, however, that, despite his commitment to aesthetic freedom, Rivière was not outlining a policy which suggested acceptance of just any literary idea or concept of literature. The director himself had definite ideas concerning the nature of artistic creation, the attitude of the artist toward his work, and the role of aesthetic activity in relation to other areas of human endeavor. As Rivière stressed in his manifesto, "Today more than ever before we intend to undertake a critical project . . . to discern, to choose, to recommend" (*NE,* 289). He had precise ideas about what he felt were valid creations and fully intended to exercise his authority as director to encourage those diverse authors whose works came closest to the ideal of excellence on which the *NRF* was founded. Rivière's own vision was somewhat limited by his unswerving belief in the necessity for renewing the principles of the French Classical tradition. But since the basis for his convictions was his desire to analyze and understand in order to arrive at truth, he was willing to listen openly to opposing points of view; he made every effort to find something worthwhile even in attitudes that were far removed from his cherished Classical ideal of purity of vision and precision of expression.

Along with providing a forum for literary exchange, the *NRF* as Rivière envisaged it would, for the first time, take an active interest in politics. Although it was not, specifically speaking, a political review, Rivière strongly felt that the *NRF* had to confront the radical changes taking place in Europe and offer "a kind of criticism and interpretation of contemporary history" (*NE*, 292). Literary and political issues had to be kept separate, but open discussions of both kinds of concerns were vital to European reconstruction, and both deserved to be presented in the pages of the *NRF*. As Rivière had come to realize during the last months of his captivity, he could no longer sit back and observe passively what was taking place in the political and social spheres. Neutrality concerning specific political issues would constitute a betrayal of the *NRF*'s general commitment to intellectual awareness and responsibility.

The project of intense analysis, informed criticism, and energetic affirmation which Rivière outlined for the *NRF* in his manifesto was at once broader and more specific than the program described by the review's founders, and it elicited much heated controversy on the part of the original editorial committee. The first to take up the gauntlet was Gide's brother-in-law Michel Arnauld, although his comments are relatively minor in comparison to others that would follow. In the very next issue of the *NRF*, he criticized Rivière's choice of the term "gratuitousness" to describe artistic freedom. He insisted that no artistic creation could be gratuituous or completely independent from any exterior influences and proposed the term "autonomous" as a substitution. He also contested Rivière's belief that the war had already dominated French minds for too long and that such domination represented a form of intellectual servitude. Instead of France's trying to forget the war as Rivière urged, Arnauld wished to preserve the memory of those years, for they would be forgotten all too quickly in their own time and the benefit that could be gained by reflecting on them lost forever. "This is the time for bearing witness to it [the war]. . . ."[7] And he went on to say that Rivière himself would not refuse to publish a work dealing with the war experience simply because it dealt with the war, concluding that "There is no source [of inspiration] already so pure that art doesn't have to clarify it each time nor any source so impure that art cannot refine it."[8] To a certain extent, Arnauld's criticism revolves around a question of vocabulary. Although

Rivière used the term "gratuitous" in his article, there is not even the vaguest hint at personal irresponsibility or any implication that artistic creation should be free from all exterior influences, in which case it would be totally subjective and the exact opposite of what Rivière admired in aesthetic activity. As he clearly stated in his lead article, he was simply emphasizing the need to free inspiration from imposed restraints and preconceived notions and allow the artist's imagination to embark on the adventure of creation through spontaneous contact with the world around him. If Rivière chose the extreme word "gratuitous" rather than "autonomous" it was precisely because he was struck by the urgency of the situation and was striving to emphasize both the importance of independence for the artist and the need for the critic to evaluate a work on its intrinsic qualities. As far as the psychological effects of the war were concerned, Rivière was quite definitely at odds with Arnauld and believed that only by passing beyond the sphere of its immediate influence could any authentic renewal take place. But this was their only area of real disagreement.

As Arnauld himself stated, Rivière would never automatically reject literary works dealing with the war; he would agree with the comments Arnauld made in his conclusion concerning the fact that there are really no impure sources of inspiration as such. In many respects, Arnauld and Rivière shared very similar ideals. They were, for the most part, speaking along parallel rather than conflicting lines, and one could legitimately consider Arnauld's "explications" as an addendum to Rivière's lead article, rather than a manifestation of deep dissension.

The disagreement between Rivière and two of the other founders, however, was of a much more serious nature. It revealed largely opposing philosophical positions concerning the very definition of the term intelligence, the concept of nationalism, the relationship between nationalism and religion, and the purpose behind the *NRF* itself. Soon after the armistice was signed in November 1918, a group of left-wing intellectuals, under the initiative of two liberal authors, Romain Rolland and Henri Barbusse, published a statement denouncing the majority of contemporary French writers and accusing them of "having reduced and debased thought by having consecrated it to the service of the mother country and to the 'War of Right.' "[9] Quick to react to what they saw as a direct attack on their integrity and their commitment to their country, a group of conservative and, for the most part, Catholic writers, headed by the intransigent Henri Massis, replied with a pompous manifesto describing the efforts of the newly formed, ultraconservative "Parti de l'Intelligence." They emphasized their unrestricted allegiance to France and enthusiastically proclaimed the value of "National intelligence in the service of national interest" (*NE,* 136).

Rivière was appalled by the vengeful narrow-mindedness of such a position and by the danger inherent in such a restricted use of the term "intelligence". He not only refused to join the party or to have anything to do with its members, but he also published a scathing criticism of Massis's project in the September 1919 issue of the *NRF,* pointing out the blatant contradictions in Massis's conception of intelligence and revealing the overall repressiveness of his program. Rivière believed, probably as firmly as Massis, in the superiority of the French intellect and the subtlety of its discerning powers. He was by no means without prejudices on this point himself, but he vehemently objected to the specific way in which Massis described intelligence and the uses he prescribed for it. Massis insisted that ' "Human intelligence is made to define and to conclude . . . it is this synthesizing genius which organizes the world" ' (*NE,* 140), and, as such, it must serve the greater glory of France. The individuals who supported Massis were totally sure of what they wanted; they were completely convinced of the righteousness of their particular outlook and wished to direct all intellectual pursuits along these specific lines to uphold and strengthen the image they had formed of what France was and should be.

Rivière, for his part, rejected such a restrictive, pragmatic attitude which ran completely counter to his conception of intelligence as "the faculty which discriminates" (*NE,* 141), whose principal activity is analysis and whose ultimate goal is truth. It is "first of all the means of distinguishing what exists from what doesn't" (*NE,* 141). Only when *all* aspects of a situation have been thoroughly examined can any attempt at integration or synthesis be made. Since Massis and his followers know specifically at the outset of their search "what they want and what they don't want" (*NE,* 141), their intelligence is not really free and they can do nothing truly constructive to further the long-term cause of renewal. Unable to see beyond the narrow frame of their self-imposed blinders, they have, in Rivière's eyes, become prisoners of their own inflexible attitudes.

The next two issues of the *NRF* brought severely critical replies to Rivière's condemnation of Massis's project. In the October 1919 issue, Jean Schlumberger published an open letter to Rivière in which he reprimanded the new director for his recent declarations. He began by affirming, "If I were Catholic, I would have signed the Intelligence Party's manifesto,"[10] and went on to stress the importance of unity and cooperation during what were particularly troubled times. Under more propitious circumstances there would be no need for the kind of restraint advocated by Massis, but in the midst of postwar turmoil, the personal restrictions and pragmatic approach to intelligence that Massis sought to impose would be helpful in re-establishing social and literary order.

In the following issue, Henri Ghéon, an ardent wartime convert to Catholicism and a member of Massis's group, published his "Réflexions sur le rôle actuel de l'intelligence française," in which he, like Schlumberger, condemned both Rivière's criticism of Massis and the young director's dedication to intellectual independence. In comments very similar to Schlumberger's, Ghéon also stressed the necessity for strengthening France in the face of the political dangers posed by the still indomitable will of the Germans and the socialist government of the newly formed Soviet Union. The "Parti de l'Intelligence" was unflinching in its nationalistic commitment, but it considered this kind of total dedication vital to France's survival at this time.

There was no reconciliation possible between the beliefs professed by "Le Parti de l'Intelligence" and Rivière's own convictions and no benefit to be gained, he felt, from continuing the debate any further. As Rivière noted in a final article on the whole subject entitled "Catholicisme et nationalisme," the essential thing was "to work hard, each one with his own ideas."[11] He did, however, take one last opportunity in this same article to comment on Schlumberger's earlier statement that if he were a Catholic he would have signed the party's manifesto. Rivière insisted that he could never become a member of "Le Parti de l'Intelligence" because it represented nothing more than a continuation of the dangerously reactionary ideas of the Action Française group. Despite its religious pretentions, this organization was totally anti-Catholic in its nationalistic idolatry and appealed to the most narrow-minded aspects of human nature. Rivière once again emphasized his distrust of absolutes and condemned the use of religious terminology to sanction intolerance.

Another very important aspect of his comments in this article is that they indicate the nature of his own commitment to Christianity. In a letter to Isabelle written a year earlier, Rivière had spoken openly of his religious convictions and the impressions which some of the founders had concerning his faith. "[Jean Schlumberger] seems to believe that I have abandoned the position which I held at the time that I wrote my article on faith. On the contrary, I still hold to it. It is to the extent that I feel myself Christian that I oppose Ghéon's point of view. I don't want to serve any idol."[12] He in no way rejected the faith which had blossomed during the time of his captivity. And in his reply to Ghéon in November 1919, Rivière affirmed the same attitude he had described in his letter to Isabelle a year earlier; "The wrongdoing of others, even of my friends, 'is quite important to me,' and I would wish that it could be avoided. It is in this way that I feel myself Christian, that I consider myself a Catholic" (NE, 144). With the responsibilities of the NRF willingly accepted and now heavy upon his shoulders, Rivière had no time and probably no desire to indulge in the kind of mystical meditation which occupied him during his years as a prisoner of war. After the war Rivière's spiritual commitment revealed itself mainly through his concern for his fellow men, his struggle against prejudice and fanaticism of all sorts, and his open-mindedness as director of the *NRF.* Though he ceased to practice Catholicism and refused to discuss religious issues, even with close friends, he nevertheless continued to live on a day-to-day basis according to the ideals that he had so eloquently described in his war journal and the convictions he had so painstakingly outlined in *A la Trace de Dieu.*

Despite the opposition from some of the review's founders and attacks from other religious and political reactionaries, Rivière unflinchingly held his ground and continued to strive for understanding and fairness in the political arena. During the six-year term of his directorship, Rivière from time to time had to deal with a number of pressing political problems, and his various articles on political issues published in the *NRF* clearly reveal the accuracy of his insight and the firmness of his conviction concerning the importance of developing a truly European community. His essays on such delicate issues as German war reparations and the occupation of the Ruhr are the efforts of a deeply concerned intellectual striving for reconciliation and international cooperation. His ideas were extremely important during a period dominated all too frequently by the desire for revenge and the inability to see beyond the borders of one's own country. And the numerous political articles which Rivière contributed to the newspaper *Luxemburger Zeitung* from late 1922 until the time of his death reiterate the same convictions as his *NRF* articles. Just as when dealing with literary issues, Rivière strove to see clearly, to understand all aspects of the problems, and to outline a course of action which, based on tolerance and acceptance of one's responsibilities, suggested guarded optimism for the future.

The subtlest and the most distressing personal and political criticism which Rivière encountered in the early years of his directorship came from Gide himself. Although he had relinquished the directorship of the *NRF* to Rivière, Gide nevertheless did not wish to give up his behind-the-scenes authority. His involvement with the review represented one of the few constants in his life, and it seemed as if this very important source of stability were slipping away from his at a time when he needed

it most. [13] Gide reacted angrily to Rivière's editorial firmness and
to the aggressive way in which he assumed control of the review.
At one point Gide even went so far as to write to Rivière insisting
that "The more I continue, the more I regret that we did not
venture to maintain the first arrangement that we had adopted:
with myself as director and you as secretary we would have done
an excellent job together—and certain of your affirmations would
have lost the aggressive character they assumed coming from the
mouth of *a director.*"[14] Gide objected, for example, to what he
saw as Rivière's overly enthusiastic praise of the value of the
Classical tradition and his extreme personal dedication to the
ideal of aesthetic purity. He also complained about what he felt
was the overly ideological nature of many of the *NRF* articles;
through his series entitled "Billets à Angèle," he explained his
reactions to various literary issues and expressed his own opinions
concerning the journal's shortcomings in the pages of the *NRF*
itself.

The remarks in the "Billet à Angèle" which appeared in the
April 1921 issue of the *NRF* reveal the extent of Gide's bitterness
and frustration over the whole directorship problem, although
his criticism of Rivière remains broad and indirect. The controversy surrounding the publication of this particular article and
the disagreements between Rivière and Gide in general after the
war are extremely complicated problems which Kevin O'Neill
has very clearly explained in his invaluable essay on the Gide-
Rivière friendship which appeared in the *Cahiers du 20ᵉ siècle.*
The years immediately following the war were a particularly
sensitive time for both men. Gide was going through the most
difficult period of his career when he felt that he had lost all of
the greatly valued sources of stability in his life, and Rivière was
eagerly seeking to establish what he felt had to be the exclusivity
of his authority as director. As O'Neill notes in his concluding
remarks, "Each one found the means to express in 1920 and 1921
his accumulated complaints against the other—and this being
done, to be rid of them."[15] Gide was able to regain his sense of
personal equilibrium and turned his full attention to work on *Les
Faux-Monnayeurs,* while Rivière devoted himself to the arduous

responsibility of the review. The two men were not only able to reestablish their former closeness, but their relationship grew in the process, for, as O'Neill further emphasizes, "From 1922 on, it was a friendship of mature men, each one going his own way and, doing this, respectful henceforth of the path which the other had chosen."[16]

Rivière and Proust

In much the same direct, resolute way that he asserted the *NRF*'s general editorial policy and defended the need for European political cooperation in the face of a rigidly nationalistic outlook, Rivière strove to make the originality of Marcel Proust's work known to European literary circles. Rivière's initial contact with Proust occurred before the war. The first volume of *A la Recherche du temps perdu*, accepted by the publishing firm of Bernard Grasset, appeared in November 1913. Proust had originally sent the manuscript of this volume, entitled *Du Côté de chez Swann*, to the *NRF* publishing division, which had been organized in 1911 through the efforts of Gide, Schlumberger, and Gaston Gallimard. Acting on the recommendation of Gide, who unfortunately had only leafed casually through the manuscript, the editorial board rejected Proust's work outright because of its length, its convoluted style, and also because of Gide's prejudice against Proust, whom he considered to be little more than a snobbish literary dilettante.

Rivière, for his part, discovered the work soon after its publication. It had been recommended to him by one of the members of the editorial team, Henri Ghéon. Although Ghéon had gone along with Gide's decision not to accept the manuscript, he was nevertheless sufficiently impressed with the work to urge Rivière to read it. When he did so, he could hardly contain his excitement. Rivière reacted with great enthusiasm, inspired by the inherent richness of the text itself and also by the correspondence between the anguish-ridden drama depicted in the section entitled *Un Amour de Swann* and his own psychological situation at the time. As Kevin O'Neill notes in his discussion of Rivière's early attraction to Proust, "At the moment that he read *Du Côté de chez Swann,* he found himself in almost exactly the same situation as Swann with Odette de Crécy so that this reading triggered in him a passionate commitment to Proust's work."[17]

Rivière was so excited about Proust's creation that he urged Gide to reexamine the book, insisting that it was worthy of his careful attention. Once Gide actually took the time to read *Du Côté de chez Swann,* he quickly recognized the stupidity of his decision not to publish it, for, as he explained to Proust in a letter of profound apology, " 'The rejection of this book will always be the greatest blunder made by the *NRF.*' "[18] Gide tried to regain Proust's confidence and strove to keep the doors open for future collaboration, but Proust's sensitive ego had been severely wounded. Although flattered by Gide's letter, he needed much prodding and gentle encouragement, such as the kind Rivière was able to provide, before he granted the *NRF* exclusive publishing rights for the whole of *A la Recherche du temps perdu.*

In January 1914 Henri Ghéon reviewed *Du Côté de chez Swann* for the *NRF.* As Kevin O'Neill points out in his explanation of the controversy surrounding the publication of Proust's manuscript, Ghéon's article is decidedly ambivalent. He appeared to be torn between his own convictions concerning the richness and the revolutionary quality of the work and his duty to justify the *NRF*'s refusal of Proust's manuscript. In his effort to explain the decision, Ghéon emphasized that it was a highly confused work, lacking in direction and aesthetic discipline.[19] When Rivière read Ghéon's review, he quickly wrote to Proust expressing his displeasure over Ghéon's description of the work as a frivolous text for leisure time reading and outlining his own reaction to Proust's literary enterprise. Unfortunately this letter has never been found, and the only clues we have concerning its specific contents come from Proust's reply dated 7 February 1914. Deeply touched by Rivière's sensitive comments Proust replied enthusiastically, "Finally I find a reader who discerns that my book is a speculative work and a construction."[20] Proust was greatly impressed with the young man's literary acuity and his concern for the undertaking that constituted his own reason for living.

This initial exchange of letters, written early in 1914, marked the beginning of a cooperative professional effort and friendship that would continue to develop until the time of Proust's death nearly nine years later. The extensive published correspondence between Proust and Rivière, most of which dates from April 1919 to early November 1922, a few weeks before Proust died, traces the course of their personal relationship, which grew to the point that Proust considered Rivière "the friend whom he places at the highest point of his intellectual and moral esteem."[21] The letters contain detailed information concerning the genesis of *A la Recherche du temps perdu* and provide an invaluable introduction to Rivière's critical study of Proust's epic undertaking. The correspondence deals, to a great extent, with the mundane particulars that make up the day-to-day routine of a publishing project, discussing, for example, deadline restrictions, printing errors, and editorial changes. Because of Proust's severe physical disabilities and Rivière's often frantic schedule at the *NRF,* the two men were rarely able to meet in person to discuss the immense project on which they were collaborating; their letters had to provide all of the information pertinent to the publication of Proust's work.

Interspersed at fairly frequent intervals among these purely professional exchanges, however, we find deeply personal expressions of respect and affection which reveal the extent of their concern for one another. The friendship between Proust and Rivière was quite different from anything Rivière had yet experienced with writers a generation older than himself. It was not, as was his friendship with Claudel, a relationship between an imposing authority figure and a somewhat errant youth. Nor did it resemble the complicated rapport which existed between himself and Gide, who had done so much to help Rivière develop his abilities to the fullest. The friendship between Rivière and Proust first developed, as had Rivière's relationship with both Claudel and Gide, from his enthusiasm for Proust's work. But despite their difference in age and the admiration which Rivière felt for Proust's creative genius, the two men were, from the beginning, equals. It was through Rivière's early expressions of confidence in Proust's ability and through his persistent efforts with the editorial board that the *NRF* publishing house eventually won Proust's trust, and after the war Rivière worked diligently to make sure that the publishing process went along as smoothly as possible for him.

At the same time it should also be noted that Rivière would not let Proust bully him. Rivière would at times become extremely irritated with Proust's incessant complaints over even the most mildly unfavorable remarks concerning his work which appeared in the *NRF*.[22] Rivière was also unflinching in his editorial decisions concerning, for example, the choice of excerpts to be printed in the *NRF*. He was sure of the accuracy of his judgment and of the fact that the passages he had decided upon were the ones that would best highlight the originality and the subtlety of Proust's vision. He likewise refused to be influenced by friendship when dealing with Proust's young protégés, such as Sidney Schiff and Jacques Porel, whose works the older man recommended to him for publication. Rivière was eager to assist any struggling, unknown writer in whatever way he could, but he could not accept what he believed to be inferior works simply because the authors of these texts came to him with Proust's recommendation. Proust, for his part, respected Rivière's authority and, most of the time, accepted his decisions with a minimal amount of complaint.

The friendship between the two men centered around their mutual esteem for one another's professional ability, but they were also intimately concerned with each other's personal welfare. They often discussed and offered advice concerning their respective physical problems, such as Proust's more and more serious asthma attacks and Rivière's nagging, nervous anxiety. From time to time Rivière also mentioned his financial difficulties to Proust and, quite unexpectedly, received in return generous offers of assistance. For example, Proust spoke in favor of Rivière with the nominating committee so that Rivière received the Prix Blumenthal in the fall of 1920, which helped alleviate his financial problems.[23] And it was through Proust's encouragement that Rivière was eventually able to rework and finally publish the long-neglected text of *Aimée.* Their personal exchanges were always simple, direct, and, in general, subdued. There was none of the adolescent melodrama and psychological intensity that frequently characterized Rivière's letters to Claudel and Gide. His intimacy with Proust was much narrower and less grandiose in scope. But, at the same time, their relationship was much more balanced than his earlier friendship with either Claudel or Gide, and the moderation of their rapport reflected Rivière's attitude toward literature and life in general after the war.

The excitement and sense of awesome discovery with which Rivière had greeted *Du Côté de chez Swann* in 1914 was the first step in his effort to define the specific originality of Proust's imagination. The previous year he had published his pivotal, synthesizing essay on *le roman d'aventure,* and, in many ways, Proust's work corresponded to the ideal of the "psychological adventure novel" (*NE,* 274) so carefully described in his article. Rivière did not notice any specific link between *Du Côté de chez Swann* and his essay at first, perhaps because of the psychological trauma he was experiencing at the time and the fact that his attention was focused very specifically on Proust's attitude toward love as depicted in *Un Amour de Swann.* But as we shall see, many of the key concepts concerning the evolution of the novel which he developed on an abstract level in his article on *le roman d'aventure* are reaffirmed in concrete terms in his postwar discussions of Proust's work.[24] Here at last was a novelist who, inspired by his passionate curiosity to understand himself and everything around him, could capture the richness of man's psychic life and communicate a feeling of plenitude to the reader in clear, crystalline form. To a great extent Proust fulfilled the description of the twentieth-century novelist which Rivière had outlined in his prewar article because he seemed to be living and writing in a state of anticipation and adventurous discovery. "He is in front of his work as he is in front of the world" (*NE,* 266). Proust advances very slowly in his effort to construct a coherent whole out of the marvels that attract his attention, and each step, each convoluted sentence he composes brings him a bit closer to his goal.

When we consider the length and complexity of Proust's literary undertaking and the extent of Rivière's admiration for it, it is quite understandable that Rivière wished to write an incisive, in-depth analysis which would mirror the vastness and the precision of the text itself. Unfortunately, Rivière was unable to carry out this long-term project because of his pressing editorial duties and because he himself died two years before the publication of *Le Temps retrouvé*, the last volume of Proust's work which explained the final stages in the protagonist's development. The only publications which Rivière had time to complete were two introductory articles describing Proust's overall innovativeness from two different points of view for the February 1920 and the January 1923 issues of the *NRF* and a series of lectures presented both in France and in Switzerland in 1923 and 1924, later published under the title *Quelques progrès dans l'étude du coeur humain.*

Rivière's investigation of Proust's creation revolves around three sets of comparisons: between Proust and the French Classicists, Proust and the nineteenth-century Positivists, and Proust and Freud. Taken together, these comparisons seek to reveal the specific nature of Proust's originality and indicate the synthesizing quality of his inspiration, which Rivière saw as capable of uniting scientific and literary concerns and of integrating the past with the present. In the first of his articles, Rivière concentrates on the relationship between Proust's art and the principles of French Classicism. Proust reacts against the lyrical imprecision that characterized the nineteenth-century novel from the time of Stendhal in the 1830s onward and culminated in the delicate introspectiveness of Symbolist-inspired prose works. He turns his attention to examining with painstaking detail and ruthless objectivity the labyrinthine paths of human emotions in an effort to reveal the truth hidden beneath our psychological camouflage. Proust tries to understand others in the same way that he tries to understand himself, and, "It is by understanding, it is by analysis, it is by knowledge that he gradually gives birth to individualized characters" (*NE,* 154). Rivière is careful to use the term "invention" rather than "creation" in this article when referring to Proust's work because Proust describes things he discovers either in himself or in the world around him. His task is much more modest than that of a creator. He begins with himself and works outward, analyzing his discoveries along the way and eventually constructing a vast, coherent network of highly individualized characters whom the reader can approach from many different angles and understand completely. Proust also reaffirms the importance of the intellect and its organizing capability as an integral part of the human personality, thereby focusing literature in the direction of understanding, the activity which Rivière valued above all others in literature as well as in everyday life because of the way in which it enabled an individual to remain flexible and continue to grow.

In his second article on *A la Recherche du temps perdu,* which appeared in the "In Memoriam" issue of the *NRF* dedicated to Proust, Rivière again affirms the link between Proust's concern for truth and precision and that of the French Classicists and suggests some of the ideas he would later develop concerning the relationship between Proust's vision of the human personality and Freud's. But in this article he pays special attention to the similarities between Proust's method and that of the late nineteenth-century Positivists. Like a dedicated scientist, Proust examines everything his gaze encounters without imposing any judgment or offering any justification for what he discovers. He destroys long-accepted theories about the nature of human motivation, depicting a world full of disconcerting surprises, "more picturesque than the one that Jules Verne had discovered at the center of the earth" (*NE,* 209). Profoundly suspicious of all appearances, Proust probes for the truth and is content merely to record his discoveries. Rivière tosses out a number of tantalizing ideas in this article, but he fails to develop any one of them sufficiently, leaving the reader in a state of somewhat frustrated expectancy. He also paints a much narrower picture of Proust's undertaking than he had in his initial article, emphasizing that Proust does not seek to proceed beyond the level of inspection and notation. He insists so strongly on the scientific aspect of Proust's analysis to the exclusion of other qualities that we run the risk of forgetting that Proust is, after all, a creative writer, not a laboratory researcher.

The scientific terminology and approach which dominated Rivière's "In Memoriam" article continue to play an extremely important role in his four-part lecture series dealing specifically with the relationship between Freud's theories about the subconscious and Proust's own explorations of human motivation. But Rivière compensates for the inadequacies of his earlier discussion by presenting a much more detailed and complete analysis of the situation and by once again stressing the aesthetic dimension of Proust's undertaking.

In his opening lecture, Rivière specifies the limits of his investigation and establishes the basis for his comparison by resuming what he considers to be the three main points of Freud's then revolutionary discoveries concerning the makeup of the human psyche: his specific definition of what the subconscious is, his theory of psychological repression and the importance of dream symbolism as related to it, and his hypothesis concerning the influence of the libido on human actions. Although Freud by no means discovered the subconscious, he was, nevertheless, the first to isolate it as a distinct psychic area, "as a domain or a realm which can be explored by using consciousness as a point of departure."[25] Consciousness, Rivière continued, is the door that leads to the secret domain of the subconscious, which contains the data necessary to understand the workings of the psyche as a whole. But because of the protective shield or disguise that consciousness draws around itself in order to adapt to exterior reality, the subconscious can be reached, deciphered, and understood only "by a patient and complicated process of inference."[26] One of the most effective ways of trying to comprehend the workings of the subconscious is through the sensitive, flexible interpretation of dreams—one of the most significant manifestations of subconscious activity. Consciousness is essentially hypocritical, substituting morally and socially acceptable actions for the spontaneous but often unacceptable ones dictated by the subconscious. The area of human conduct in which such camouflaging occurs most frequently is in the realm of sexuality.

This brings Rivière to the third aspect of Freud's originality, his revelations about the role of the sexual instinct or libido in the organization of the subconscious. Rivière underlines the ambiguity surrounding this concept as it appears in Freud's analyses, since the term sometimes refers merely to sexual desire and, at others, takes on a quasi-metaphysical connotation. But he also indicates his own general acceptance of Freud's theories about the importance of the instinct by affirming that "The idea of desire as the motivating force of all our expansive activity appears to me to be an admirably innovative truth."[27] Rivière also points out how Freud's stress on the importance of the libido leads to a totally subjectivist concept of love. An individual is moved not by the qualities inherent in another, but by the secret force of his own desire, which conditions his reactions to others. And in his conclusion, when describing the overall significance of Freud's contribution, Rivière emphasizes that Freud not only discovered a new realm for scientific investigation (that of the subconscious) and revealed the ways in which consciousness camouflages it, but he also developed a new, inductive method for decoding the signs of the subconscious. He created a method which "gives intelligence an active role . . . of caution and penetration which . . . has always been the only [role] which makes understanding possible."[28] Working slowly and carefully, intelligence can sort out and transform the complicated and often confused data presented by the subconscious into patterns which can begin to reveal the truth about our motivations.

In his second lecture, entitled "Marcel Proust, l'Inconscient dans son oeuvre," Rivière turns his attention to Proust's masterpiece and begins the task of trying to define the kind of relationship or similarity which exists between Freud's theories and the principles behind Proust's monumental literary project. He is careful to point out at the very beginning that the two men were working with totally different purposes in mind—Freud being a scientist and Proust a creative writer. Rivière further insists that it is impossible to speak of any direct influence since Proust knew nothing of Freud's ideas. Nevertheless, like Freud in his scientific investigations, Proust utilizes the subtle force of his intelligence to decipher the hidden meaning behind human actions, to examine objectively the totally subjective nature of the psyche. Proust was obsessed by the desire for absolute truth and at first set out to discover everything possible about the world. But he was soon discouraged by the illusory quality of the things around him and finally turned his attention to the only reality about which he could be certain—that of his own personality. As Rivière emphasizes, "It is himself as a system of perceptions, of emotions and of ideas that he is going to propose as the object of his study."[29] He seeks to examine in minute detail the mass of often contradictory perceptions swirling within him and, through his investigations, to explain the structure, not only of his psyche, but of the human personality in general.

In much the same way as Freud, Proust also conceives of the subconscious as a distinct, multi-leveled realm to be understood in relation to consciousness. And, in Rivière's eyes, he is the first *writer* to demonstrate the structural complexity of the psyche. Proust's gaze, like Freud's, is free from all moral inhibitions. It goes everywhere, ruthlessly exposing the secret motivational forces at work behind the hypocritical façade of consciousness. But, despite their many resemblances, Rivière feels that Proust is even more radical and more subversive than Freud when he begins to define the nature of man's psychic complexity. In contrast to Freud, who emphasized the dynamic or reciprocal relationship between the conscious and the subconscious, Proust indicates that the two realms are simply parallel and can never really interact. It is precisely this attitude which is the source of "his terrible originality."[30] Proust rejects the idea of the integrity or completeness of the personality, mercilessly exposing the irremediable fragmentation of human identity. The only kind of unity which exists is the simple, superficial unity of physical presence. In one individual there is not one personality but many, each of which exists in *total* solitude and comes briefly to the fore only when stirred by some chance occurrence or outside catalyst. These moments of psychological illumination, which Proust calls "intermittences of the heart," occur when characters are aroused by, for example, the taste of a madeleine, the theme from a

Vinteuil sonata or a return visit to Balbec. But the sensation of plenitude which they bring is only temporary and disappears as soon as the catalyst itself fades away.

The ramifications of this fragmented view of the personality are particularly disconcerting in relation to Proust's theory of love, which Rivière examines in his third lecture, entitled "Marcel Proust et l'esprit positif." He recapitulates the remarks made in his earlier article concerning the similarities between Proust's method and that of the scientific Positivists, insisting that at the basis of Proust's undertaking is "the pure and simple task of describing . . . of subordinating explanation to observation."[31] His gaze is ruthless and all-penetrating in seeking out the truth that we so desperately try to hide from ourselves. And, in Rivière's eyes, the most painful, most destructive revelation Proust makes about human emotions concerns the subjective quality of love. What we feel for others is totally dependent on our own disposition. It is precisely our very intense suffering as solitary, fragmented creatures which makes us so vulnerable to the illusions of love and triggers our attraction to an equally lonely, equally tormented being. Thus Proust arrives at the reversal of generally accepted notions about the genesis of an individual's interest in another person by revealing "that sorrow is the cause of love. . . ."[32] He unveils what he sees as the pathetic hypocrisy of all human relations, shattering even the most persistent of our illusions.

The third lecture ends with Rivière affirming the boldness of Proust's undertaking and indicating his overall acceptance of Proust's radical ideas. But in his fourth and final lecture, Rivière examines the issue from a slightly different point of view. He attempts to measure the degree of truth in Proust's conclusions while at the same time explaining in greater detail his own reactions to certain of Proust's attitudes. For the most part, Rivière is in agreement with Proust's image of the human psyche. But he insists that Proust is too extreme in his pessimism and in his inability to admit that the desire to give of oneself also plays an important part in a love relationship. Rivière likewise believes that Proust is perhaps too suspicious of human motivations and that he goes too far with his theory of impenetrable solitude. By emphasizing the complete separation of the various layers of the psyche from one another, Proust "eliminates the dramatic element from consciousness."[33] He suppresses the possibility of authentic interaction between characters, which can lead ultimately to what Rivière describes as the "disappearance of the being who acts behind the being who perceives, who thinks,"[34] the same kind of situation he had described so many years before in "De la Sincérité envers soi-même." Even this shortcoming, however, is fairly insignificant, Rivière feels, when compared to the enormity of Proust's psychological discoveries. More than any other novelist before him, he both unmasks the forces of the subconscious and triumphs over these forces through the power of his intelligence, which discerns the layered complexity of man's psychic makeup and explains it through the creation of a work of art.

Proust, Rivière concludes, manages to combine the analytical principles of French Classicism with nineteenth-century research techniques and a revolutionary conception of the human personality, thereby creating a unique synthesis of the past and the present. For all his effort to reveal the integrating aspect of Proust's inspiration, however, Rivière's study ends up falling somewhat short of its goal. The discussion of the similarities between Proust and Freud constitutes the most illuminating, most innovative, and most critically daring section of his analysis. The parallels Rivière draws between the two men's description of the psyche reveal the radical modernity of Proust's vision and emphasize Rivière's own openness toward some of the most startling twentieth-century scientific theories.

Nevertheless, in each of his discussions of Proust's undertaking, Rivière seems to insist a bit too exclusively on the brutally destructive aspect of Proust's inspiration and to overemphasize the strictly scientific and intellectual qualities of his explorations. The image he presents of Proust is very enlightening, but rather limited because of this. Although Proust refuses to judge his characters on the basis of moral prerogatives, he is nonetheless striving to reveal more than a scientific or even a purely intellectual truth. Like Vinteuil's musical phrase, described so poignantly in *Du Côté de chez Swann*—a passage which Rivière cites but does not elaborate upon at the end of his lecture series—Proust's work triumphs, in a sense, over human mortality as well as over the subconscious. And through the boldness of his explorations, Proust has opened the door to even more radical, more surprising forms of psychological adventure and literary investigation.

In order to be fair to Rivière, however, one final remark must be added concerning his analysis of Proust's work. Rivière first presented his four-part lecture series on Proust at the Vieux-Colombier theater in Paris in January 1923. A little over a year later, in March 1924, he presented a single lecture on Proust in Monaco. This latter work is, for the most part, a résumé of the principal points he had stressed the year before. In his concluding remarks Rivière again cites the passage from *Du Côté de chez Swann* where Swann listens to Vinteuil's musical phrase in the salon of the Duchesse de Saint Euverte. But instead of ending with the quotation itself, he comments on the way in which Proust has revealed the richness *(richesse)* of the human soul *(âme)*. He stresses once again the importance of the intellect in Proust's creation, but he also goes a bit further when he notes in the last paragraph:

His [Proust's] sensibility has taken on an eternal value. It escapes from time. And an entire world which was captured with it. The great sickly individual . . . which Proust was, managed, from the confines of his bed, . . . to win the most difficult of victories: he asserted himself quite completely in the face of death, and it retreats, intimidated, when confronted with his completely preserved moral form.[35]

This kind of comment, in our opinion, complements the image of Proust which Rivière presented in his earlier lecture series. He goes much more clearly beyond the scientific and intellectual dimension to stress the aesthetic and the profoundly human universality of Proust's undertaking. Proust may have ignored traditional definitions of morality, but as Rivière so eloquently notes here, he was by no means insensitive or inhuman. His work constitutes an authentic artistic whole which involves all of the reader's faculties, his emotions as well as his intellect.

Rivière versus Fernandez on Moralism and Literature

Even in its unfinished state, Proust's epic creation fulfilled Rivière's dream of a Classical revival and constituted his ideal of an autonomous work free of all moral judgments. In the last two years of his life Rivière became so adamant about the need for objectivity in literature that it eventually led to a public confrontation between him and another critic who had contributed extensively to the *NRF,* Ramon Fernandez. The two men took part in a series of debates (eventually published under the title *Moralisme et littérature)* which were held in Lausanne and Geneva two months before Rivière's death. What is so paradoxical about this series of discussions is that Rivière and Fernandez are in basic agreement as to what constitutes an integrated vision of the human personality and, to a great extent, what constitutes a satisfying artistic creation. But it is only in the concluding section that this becomes clear. The debate revolves around the question as to whether or not moral considerations should play a role in literary creation. In explaining his stance on the issue, Rivière adopts a strictly psychological point of view and develops his argument around a discussion of Racine's theater. He describes in detail the penetrating exactness of Racine's dramatic portraits. "He [Racine] reveals what I would like to call the direct or pure contact of sentiments with one another, the instantaneous way in which they can be modified. No intervention from reflection or reason."[36] Rivière goes on to point out, by means of numerous examples, "the beauty and even, if I dare say so, virtue of this literature to which I have no fear of applying the epithets 'dissolute' and 'shameless.' "[37] He insists on the grandeur and the monstrous truthfulness both of Racine's psychological approach and that of the French Classicists in general who, without any moral preconceptions to obscure their vision, explored the depths of the human personality.

Rivière accuses Rousseau of having been the first in French literature to introduce a precisely moral preoccupation into psychological exploration. Rousseau set himself up as "simultaneously the narrator and the judge of his soul,"[38] and thus subverted the essential purity and the objectivity of the Classical vision. Rivière discusses at length what he feels were the disastrous effects which Rousseau's basic change in attitude and emphasis had on nineteenth-century French literature as a whole, insisting on the need to return to the directness of the Classical writers' approach: "We must now enter the realm of novelistic and dramatic fiction as enemies of all falsification, with the precision and penetration of the Classicists, with their horror for all precipitous judgments . . . with their taste for life."[39] Once again Rivière reaffirms some of the same general attitudes he had expressed more than ten years earlier in his study on the adventure novel and, more recently, in the postwar *NRF* manifesto and in his lectures on Proust.

In his detailed rebuttal to Rivière's statements, Fernandez attacks the problem from a very different vantage point and even attributes a different meaning to the term "moralism". Whereas Rivière concentrated more on the *writer's* attitude toward strictly moral concerns or attitudes, Fernandez examines the question of moral consciousness or awareness on the part of the characters themselves. He brings the debate into a different realm by indicating his intention to discuss "morality understood as an essential part of human knowledge and expression."[40] He describes what he sees as a basic moral orientation in every human being and insists that a writer must take this into consideration if he wishes to develop well-rounded, profoundly human characters. In Fernandez's opinion, it is essential that characters in a novel or play reveal some kind of moral awareness in order to be complete as individuals. Racine's characters, he insists, are incomplete as tragic heroes or heroines-because they never develop beyond the level of animal instinct. Phèdre's agony, for example, is not grandiose because it exists beneath the level of moral consciousness.[41]

He further states that as soon as a strictly psychological position is abandoned, even Racine can no longer be described as objective;

even he has specific preferences, making the choice to depict, not the kind of heroic self-mastery that Fernandez admires, but rather corrosive passions that cause the entire personality to disintegrate. In the face of this extreme kind of disintegration, Fernandez prefers even the excessive moralizing of Rousseau because "he imagines above himself,"[42] because he at least aspires to something beyond the reality of his current situation. Fernandez refers to the works of other, more contemporary French writers along with a number of English-speaking authors, such as Thomas Hardy, George Meredith, and Joseph Conrad, praising them because the characters in their creations reveal the kind of moral dimension he considers so important. In contrast he expresses his dissatisfaction with Proust's novel precisely because Proust "considers and maintains life beneath the level where the moral phenomenon appears."[43] As Fernandez emphasizes in his concluding remarks, he is speaking out for psychological plenitude and depth of characterization. He is attempting, as he puts it, "to defend the integrity of the human experience against an interpretation which, in my opinion, mutilates man while insisting that it is revealing him."[44]

In a brief concluding section appropriately entitled "Tentative de synthèse," Rivière answers some of Fernandez's assertions and tries to clear up some of the confusion which his own remarks may have caused. He feels it necessary to add a few final explanatory remarks of his own because of the way in which Fernandez altered the original issue, "I think that he altered, transformed, and deepened the question which I had posed."[45] But at the same time that he is explaining how Fernandez changed the level and the direction of the debate, Rivière is forced to acknowledge that he is in basic agreement with Fernandez's concept of what constitutes psychological plenitude. He admits that a strictly intellectual or scientific approach cannot capture the fullness of the human personality.

What is even more significant in the light of his lectures in praise of Proust's positivist method is that Rivière now emphasizes the limitations of Proust's technique. He is careful not merely to mention as he had earlier, but to emphasize that, in excitement over Proust's innovativeness, "I concealed the painful, suffocating quality which Proust's radical amoralism also at times had for me."[46] When confronted with Fernandez's rebuttal, he seems to realize that he had been rather extreme in his repeated insistence on the value of a strictly intellectual approach to literary creation and in his insistence on the purity of vision that this attitude fostered. No longer are Proust's revelations about the workings of the psyche sufficient compensation as they had previously been for the complete absence of a specific moral dimension in his epic work. In retrospect, Rivière admits that he perhaps went too far in stressing the importance of what Proust's scientific method could reveal about human nature.

Our only regret about Rivière's comments in this section of the debate is that in modifying his ideas somewhat concerning the value of a strictly intellectual approach to literary creation, he did not go a bit further and reexamine Proust's work from a slightly different, more all-inclusive point of view (as he hinted at in certain sections of his Monaco lecture) or mildly broaden his concept of moralism to include the kind of awareness and understanding that Proust described so precisely and so sensitively.

Rivière Confronts Dada and Surrealism

In spite of certain changes in his attitude toward Proust which surfaced in his discussions with Fernandez, Rivière continued to emphasize the importance of the relationship between Proust and the French Classicists and to stress the promise which the Classical concept of literature held for future aesthetic development. And this conviction greatly influenced the way in which he viewed another postwar phenomenon—that of Dadaism, which erupted in full force in France in 1919. When we consider the depth of his personal commitment to the analytical purity of the Classical vision, it is not surprising that Rivière would react negatively to the tortured cries of the Dadaists who descended upon Paris after World War I, preaching the destruction of all of Western civilization. Rivière had grown up under the influence of the Symbolists; he had not been receptive to the experimentation of the Cubist painters before the war,[47] nor, as we have seen earlier

in our study, was he drawn to the radical kind of aesthetic explorations undertaken by poets such as Guillaume Apollinaire,
Max Jacob, or Pierre Reverdy in the early twentieth century.
Furthermore, during his years in captivity, he was completely
cut off from the Paris literary scene. When he lectured on contemporary French literature in Switzerland in February 1918, the
only poets who figured in his presentation were fairly traditional
ones, such as Francis Jammes or the Unanimists, under the leadership of Jules Romains. His knowledge of current poetic trends
was, at best, painfully limited. He was, as Michel Décaudin notes
at the beginning of his article "Rivière et Dada," quite "ill-
prepared for an encounter with Dada."[48] It was only after his
return to Paris in 1918 that Rivière really began to read for the
first time the works of France's more revolutionary contemporary
poets. When he took over the directorship of the *NRF* he had
to come to grips with the whole explosive phenomenon of Dada
and take a definite stand in response to it.

The first serious significant discussion of the whole Dada issue
to appear in the pages of the *NRF* was a brief, witty, and subtly
encouraging article by Gide in April 1920. The Dadaist question
was yet another source of tension and dispute between Gide and
Rivière at this time. Gide, quite understandably, was much more
disposed to look favorably on the anarchism of the Dadaist cause
than Rivière, and their disagreement over this issue added more
fuel to their already smoldering relationship.[49] Gide's article sin-
gled out the role of foreign influences on the movement, namely
that of the Rumanian-born Tristan Tzara, the group's most violent spokesman, and emphasized the all-encompassing scope of
Dada's destructive instinct. Nevertheless, Gide was fascinated
with many aspects of the enterprise and encouraged the young
revolutionaries in their efforts to break with the past and strike
out on their own. As he put it, "I think that each new need must
create its own new form and that the present is suffering under
the weight of the past."[50]

Rivière's own response to Dada appeared several months later,
immediately following an explanatory article entitled "Pour
Dada" by André Breton, who would soon reject the complete

nihilism of the Dadaists and become the principal spokesman for Surrealism. Even though Breton was still formally associated with the Dadaists at this time, his comments in this article are already curiously affirmative. He insists that it is wrong to equate Dadaism with a totally closed, subjectivist attitude, stressing instead the overall coherence of man's psychic life on the individual and collective level. Breton likewise expresses his full agreement with those who have emphasized the relationship between Dada's explorations and those undertaken by Freud. But he also cautions against associating the Dadaists' investigations too closely with the strictly scientific experiments of Freudian psychologists, and he ends on an unusually positive note, indicating that the extreme destructiveness of the Dadaists will not last much longer. Their own instinct for self-preservation will keep them from going too far in their negation. The picture Breton sketches of Dadaism is, as Michel Décaudin appropriately points out, "a reassuring picture, apt not to shock the *NRF*'s faithful readers."[51] But even more importantly, it constitutes "a before the fact Surrealist manifesto."[52] Breton himself had already progressed beyond the purely destructive violence which animated the Dadaist effort and was laying the foundation for the collective affirmation known as Surrealism, which would gradually take shape over the next several years.

Rivière's own essay "Reconaissance à Dada," which immediately follows Breton's article, should not be considered as either an extension of Gide's commentary or a direct reply to Breton's presentation, although Rivière does express some of the same concerns as Gide and treats some of the specific issues which Breton mentions in his essay. Rivière's article is, rather, the first intelligent evaluation of the Dadaist movement as a whole, one which discusses its significance in relation to what has preceded it. As Rivière's other writings have done, this article too emphasizes the continuity of his vision and reveals his insight into both the literary significance and the consequences of the Dadaist revolt.

In the first part of his discussion, Rivière attacks what he perceives as the Dadaists substitution of uninhibited self-expression or exteriorization of impressions for artistic invention—a term which, for Rivière, denotes choice and personal discipline. In their attempt to seize and depict the primitive, prerational unity of the human psyche, the Dadaists have ended up substituting what Rivière describes as an indecipherable, absurd unity for logical coherence. They have left the realm of aesthetics and literature far behind in an attempt to capture "the experience of absolute psychological reality" (*NE, 296*). Language no longer has any fixed significance whatsoever, and the task of writing has degenerated to become "an essentially private act" (*NE, 299*). No hope remains for communication or comprehension.

In sharp contrast to Breton, Rivière sees the Dadaist attitude as being totally closed and subjective, and he feels that their verbalizations are depressingly impenetrable. In this respect, the Dadaists appear to Rivière as the most extreme manifestation of the nineteenth-century adventure in emotional expression or exteriorization; they constitute an important stage in a precisely literary evolution. And in the second part of his article, Rivière proceeds to evaluate the current Dadaist revolution in the light of what occurred during the previous century. As he had explained once before in his article on the adventure novel (and would again do so in his lectures on Proust and in his debate with Fernandez), Rivière praises the lucidity of the seventeenth-century writers and briefly outlines the gradual decline in literary objectivity which occurred in France in the nineteenth century. The tendency to stress the importance of the creative ego began with the Romantics and grew more and more intense throughout the nineteenth century. It reached a high point with the Symbolists in the late 1890s, continued into the twentieth century with the poets associated with Cubism, and has finally culminated in the absolute incoherencies of the Dadaists. Rivière is grateful to these nihilistic adventurers for having finally attained the ultimate aesthetic impasse of totally substituting instinctive expression for artistic creation. In Rivière's eyes, Dada constitutes an end point, not a new beginning. Now that it has been reached, Rivière hopes that literature can once again adopt a more modest, more limited, and more truthful attitude which stresses the effort to understand.

Rivière's article on Dada emphasized once again his lifelong preoccupation with objective truth and understanding. The Dadaists represented the epitome of an attitude which he had been opposing from the time of his own adolescence when he encountered Claudel's works and first began to recognize the rich potential to be explored in the world around him as opposed to concentrating too exclusively on the murmurings of his private dream world. In his article on Dada, Rivière grouped the major nineteenth-century and early-twentieth-century poets together in a confused mass, as if he were unable to distinguish them from one another in any significant way. He viewed them all from a single point of reference, emphasizing their concept of poetry as personal quest and did not seem to recognize the intense self-discipline and intellectual lucidity which the efforts of many of them required. Rivière's insight and degree of comprehension were limited by his commitment to the analytical purity of Classicism. But he did make every effort to treat the heated Dadaist controversy as honestly and as dispassionately as possible, which was more than any other critic did in 1920. He also understood that, for all of their protestations to the contrary, the Dadaists were nevertheless literary revolutionaries, and he was quite accurate in his assessment of Dada's basic limitations. He could see that Dada would very soon burn itself out. It was the ultimate form of destruction which had to take place before a new affirmation could occur.

Although he could say nothing really positive about the efforts of the Dadaist group who clustered around Tristan Tzara, Rivière felt somewhat differently about the poets who, in the early 1920s, formally broke with Dada to engage in the adventure of Surrealism. As a somewhat later article reveals, he was by no means categorically opposed to the kind of poetic incantations created by Breton and his fellow explorers of the absolute. In "Crise du concept de littérature," published in the *NRF* in February 1924, Rivière stressed that the current attitude of the former Dada group was much more complex than the position he had described in 1920, and he in no way sought to suppress their activities. In fact, as even a quick glance at the *NRF* from late 1920 to

1925 will indicate, Rivière welcomed their collaboration and defended them in the face of outraged criticism from more traditional authors.[53] "I am not attacking pure poetry; I seek only to limit its domain. . . . I hope that there will always be a group of individuals who have taken it upon themselves to insure our communication with the absolute. But I do not wish to allow them to impose by terror the function they have chosen as the only valid and venerable one" (*NE.* 320). He fully recognized the value and importance of the Surrealists' quest, but he did not feel that they had the right to condemn other less grandiose, less majestic forms of aesthetic activity or scorn those who disagreed with their position.

Rivière wrote his article on the meaning of the term "literature", one of the last he would ever publish in the *NRF,* in direct response to a provocative, controversial essay by the young writer Marcel Arland. Entitled "Sur un nouveau mal du siècle," it was so called because of the resemblance Arland saw between the profound disquietude of his generation and the malaise that had affected the Romantics a hundred years earlier. Arland rejected the decadence, confusion, and lack of purpose of both the recent past and the present; he insisted that literature had to be directly linked to ethical considerations and, even more specifically, to spiritual concerns. "All questions come down to a single problem, that of God, the eternal torment of men whether they are striving to create or to destroy Him."[54] He described literary creation strictly in terms of metaphysical investigation, transforming it into an all-consuming, sacred activity, which demanded total commitment on the part of the individual. Literature is not an end in itself but a means of self-possession, self-revelation, and, at times, a form of personal exorcism. In Arland's eyes, to write meant to confront and explore the depths of one's anguish and, through the very act of writing, attempt to move beyond the grasp of one's private demons. For Arland writing became a way of attaining personal salvation in an era of spiritual fragmentation.

Although they both reacted against the pointless destruction wreaked by the Dadaists, Rivière and Arland could agree on little else because they approached literature from two opposing points of view. In his reply to Arland's plea for a spiritually oriented literature which would probe the ethical dilemmas facing individuals in the twentieth century, Rivière pointed out once again the danger in subordinating literature to exterior goals and transforming it into a quasi-sacred activity with the writer as either victim or priest. The unrest afflicting the young writers in the 1920s was not, in Rivière's eyes, a *new* malaise, but, as he had already indicated in his earlier article on Dada, the continuation of the same self-centered *mal du siècle* that had tormented the Romantics. Rivière was not interested in pursuing the question of why someone would choose to write because such interrogations could lead only to extreme solutions: "At the moment when we allow our mind to pose this last question, it can only reply by religious faith or suicide" (*NE,* 319). Rivière, for his part, opted for a much more precise and at the same time more modest, more relative concept of literature, which clearly restricted its possibilities and defined its perimeters. Rivière firmly believed that a writer *must* confront the problems facing mankind, but within certain limits. He adopted a middle-of-the-road position which consisted "of taking note of certain pleasures which are possible, of pursuing them, and of allowing life to develop in us" (*NE,* 319).

From at least the time he wrote "Le Roman d'aventure" onward, Rivière had been striving to establish a concern for balance and moderation in literature, an attitude which, in his eyes, offered the most potential for artistic development. He actively committed himself to an extroverted concept of literature as discovery and understanding, which, without any moral or specifically religious pretensions, seeks to reveal the beauty and infinite complexity of even the most ordinary phenomena. And Rivière's own sense of discovery and ability to comprehend met their final and most difficult test when he encountered the inscrutable poems of the young, unknown, and deeply tormented Antonin Artaud.

Rivière Confronts the Enigma of Artaud

In the spring of 1923, the 27-year-old Antonin Artaud, who had come to Paris three years before and had been working as an

actor with the important director Charles Dullin, sent the *NRF*
collection of eight poems entitled *Tric Trac du Ciel*. Rivière refused
to publish Artaud's poems because he found them incoherent and
lacking in aesthetic unity. But he was sufficiently impressed with
their emotional intensity and the glimmers of understanding they
revealed to wish to speak to the author in person. Rivière wrote
to Artaud asking him to stop by the *NRF* offices some Friday
between 4 and 6 P.M. so that they could discuss Artaud's poems
in greater detail. Artaud came a few weeks later on 5 June 1923
and that very evening wrote Rivière a long letter in order to
elaborate further on some of the things the two men had discussed
earlier that day. These letters were the first of eleven that Rivière
and Artaud would exchange over the next year, and this brief
literary, psychological, and philosophical correspondence constitutes what the distinguished critic Maurice Blanchot has referred
to as "a greatly significant event . . ."[55] in the evolution of
twentieth-century French literature.

In asking Artaud to come to see him personally, Rivière revealed his desire to learn more about the traumatic personal drama
which inspired and gave birth to the poems; in accepting Rivière's
invitation and writing to him only a few hours after their first
meeting, Artaud revealed his need to be understood by someone
whose opinion he respected and whose psychological sensitivity
he had heard so much about. As critic Bettina Knapp aptly notes
in her discussion of the Rivière-Artaud relationship: "Each man
responded to the other and each seemed to answer some inner
need in the other."[56] Artaud wanted Rivière to be able to comprehend the depth and the uniqueness of his particular problem.
If the poems submitted to the *NRF* seemed fragmented and
incoherent to Rivière, it was because Artaud was suffering from
what he described as "a frightful illness of the spirit. My thought
abandons me at every turn. . . . When I can seize any form,
however imperfect it may be, I fix it, in the fear of losing the
entire thought."[57] The only kind of thoughts he could express
in poems were mere fragments, but he felt that these confused,
dislocated phrases, not only had the right to exist, but also
deserved to be published in a literary review because of the anguish

and suffering that went into formulating them. They were the manifestation of Artaud's impossible dream to unite life and thought in language in a moment of plenitude.

At first Rivière clearly did not comprehend either the nature or the scope of Artaud's difficulties. Given his duty as editor, he was considering Artaud's situation from a strictly aesthetic point of view in the light of the rigorous *NRF* stylistic standards and tried to assure the younger man that his case was neither as unusual nor as serious as he perceived it to be. Rivière counseled Artaud by saying that "With a little patience . . . you will manage to write perfectly coherent and harmonious poems."[58] Artaud was, quite understandably, angry with Rivière's letter and insulted by the simplistic advice the director offered. Artaud had come to Rivière because he respected him and because he sincerely felt that, as sensitive as Rivière was, he would certainly be able to grasp the severity of his own state. It took many months for Artaud's anger to subside. It was not until January 1924 that he again wrote to Rivière to try one more time to convince him of the gravity of his problem, of the kind of malevolent force which was gradually causing his entire being to disintegrate. His difficulties had nothing to do with the stylistic problem of searching for the right words to express his ideas. It was the ideas themselves that were slowly but surely being corroded at the very moment that he was trying to seize them. As Artaud put it, "There is, to be sure, something which is destroying my thought."[59] Given the nature of this disturbance, it was absurd for Rivière to offer literary platitudes instead of sympathy and sensitive insight and to insist that Artaud would be able to solve his problem in the same way that other writers could.

It took Rivière nearly two months to answer Artaud's plea for understanding. But when he finally did, his comments reveal the degree of his change in attitude toward Artaud and his anguish. This letter marks what could be rightfully called the second stage in Rivière's effort to decipher the meaning of Artaud's dilemma. He apologized for his earlier comments because he now recognized the depth of Artaud's difficulties and the fact that his entire psyche was involved. But Rivière still thought that Artaud could attain some semblance of equilibrium if he tried to channel the mental activity of which he was capable in a particular direction, rather than letting it flow unrestrained as he seemed to have done in his poems. As he did in his article "La Crise du concept de littérature," Rivière emphasized the danger in absolutist positions and the value to be gained from compromise, from adopting a more modest attitude. "There is no other outlet for pure thought than death. . . . If by thought you mean *creation*, as you seem to do most of the time, it must at all cost be relative. . . ."[60] He encouraged Artaud at least to try to direct the intellectual force he did have toward a specific object. This kind of activity, Rivière firmly believed, would alleviate at least some of Artaud's intense suffering. Rivière did not yet fully realize that Artaud's anguish was not only unique but also totally self-contained. But he knew that he was dealing with a situation which he at least had never before encountered and wished others to have the opportunity of learning about Artaud and his struggle. It was at this point in their correspondence that Rivière suggested publishing their exchanges as a series of imaginary letters. Artaud eagerly agreed to Rivière's idea as long as their correspondence was presented as a true story, not fiction. It was his very life that he had been describing so agonizingly to Rivière over the past eleven months, and he wanted the *NRF* readers to know without any doubt that his problems were real.

In his last two letters to Rivière, Artaud went even further in his efforts to pinpoint the kind of malady plaguing him. In reply to Rivière's advice about channeling his thoughts, he insisted that he was incapable of doing so because of an "overwhelming physiological weakness."[61] He was suffering from physical and mental paralysis which prevented him from concentrating on anything at all outside himself, much less anything specific. Artaud also stressed the difference between his own case and that of other poets such as Tristan Tzara, André Breton, and Pierre Reverdy, who, despite their anguish, never lost control of themselves in their poetic explorations. As Artaud was careful to point out, "It remains that they do not suffer and that I suffer, not only in my mind [*esprit*] but in my flesh and in my soul [*âme*]. . . ."[62] His situation was, he felt, the most desperate case that could be imagined.

Rivière, for his part, finally came to realize the exclusivity of Artaud's situation. In his last letters to Rivière, Artaud first added and then substituted the word soul for mind. This change, coupled with Artaud's more detailed explanations, helped Rivière realize the completely overwhelming, metaphysical quality of his misery. As Rivière admitted in his final letter to the tortured young man, "I feel it, I am touching upon a profound and *private* [our emphasis] anguish."[63] He was able to understand the desperation of Artaud's position as well as another human being ever could. Rivière emphasized that there were certain similarities between Artaud's troubles and his own problem of at times feeling himself desperately inferior, of being unable to realize his full potential. But he also acknowledged that he never experienced the sense of disintegration or total helplessness that Artaud had to endure. As Rivière put it, "I do not even in moments of intense anguish lose . . . all idea of my complete reality. . . ."[64] Rivière was too passionately committed to life to lose himself in the kind of self-contained torture that consumed Artaud.

Many years before, he had spelled out the dangers of absolute sincerity and renounced it in favor of a more relative attitude which allowed for change and psychological growth. In a similar way did he reject the impasse which Artaud's position exemplified. As Naomi Greene explains in her analysis of Artaud's enigmatic condition, Artaud wanted to be fully aware of and, in a sense, to possess his thoughts as he was thinking them. "But since thoughts are not physical objects, it is evident that . . . Artaud is reaching for the impossible. For, if thought is to be aware of itself, it cannot at the same time be concerned with exterior ideas or emotions. If it is always turned inward, always preoccupied with its own existence, it cannot 'think' about other things. This would preclude all mental functions."[65] Artaud's attempt to possess his thoughts was as self-destructive as the concept of total sincerity and could end only in madness and death.

Rivière arrived at the point where he could comprehend the nature and unique degree of Artaud's anguish, and he clearly saw where it would eventually lead. But in the midst of Artaud's intense suffering, Rivière could also discern the power of Artaud's will, the strength of his ability to resist, and the depth of his desire for human contact. These forces had moved Artaud to write to Rivière in the first place, and they could perhaps help him break out of the circle of his torture. One last time Rivière, in spite of himself as he put it, tried to offer Artaud some hope. In his own life, Rivière refused to yield in any struggle, insisting that "There is absolute peril only for him who abandons himself; there is complete death only for him who develops a liking for dying."[66] He begged Artaud to continue struggling, for as long as he struggled, the danger of total disintegration was not irremediable. And the letters exchanged between the two men in 1923 and 1924, which reveal their individual attitudes toward literary creation and life in general, constitute one of the most illuminating documents for anyone trying to comprehend the different directions French literature has taken since Rivière's time, when the kind of anguish that tormented Artaud would no longer be as unique as it seemed to be in the early 1920s.

Despite Rivière's passionate commitment to life, the ultimate confrontation which he spoke of to Artaud, came for him only eight months after he last wrote to the young man, revealing his insight into Artaud's anguish and expressing his profound compassion. During the last months of his life, Rivière worked whenever he could on an important personal manuscript entitled *Florence,* which was to be his second novel.[67] As director of the *NRF* he kept fighting as fiercely as ever for tolerance, understanding, and moderation. He defended both Gide and the whole *NRF* undertaking against Massis's attacks. He debated the sensitive issue of moralism and literature with Fernandez, emphasizing the need for literary works to reveal the truth about characters, no matter how reprehensible those revelations might be. He continued to speak out in favor of a concept of literature that embraces all of the contradictions and paradoxes that make up human life. At the same time, he refused to let literary creation become itself an absolute—an occurrence which he felt could only lead to the death of literature itself and to destruction of the beauty and knowledge it could bring to human beings.

Chapter Seven

Conclusion

When Jacques Rivière died on 14 February 1925, he left behind a literary legacy dedicated to the ideals of truth and understanding and inspired by the passionate commitment of living every moment to the fullest. His vast repertoire of critical writings on complex literary issues as well as on music and art constitutes one of the essential elements in the development of contemporary French criticism. Rivière was one of the first in the early twentieth century to view literary criticism as intense interaction between the critic and the text. Rejecting the mechanistic approach of Hippolyte Taine, the biographical method of Sainte-Beuve, and the exaggerated erudition of Gustave Lanson, he endeavored to concentrate upon the intricacies of the works themselves. Rivière responded both emotionally and intellectually to aesthetic works and drew upon both of these forces, first, to experience the work as fully as possible, and then to explain in detail the complexity of the psychological and stylistic phenomena which structured the text under consideration. His mental suppleness enabled him to get as close as possible to specific works without distorting them and to define clearly and accurately the terms of a particular author's attitude toward life. Because of the sensitivity and precision of his critical analyses, he could reveal the unity and originality of the author's vision and make his works live in a new way for others. Throughout his life, Rivière was animated by the passion for discovery and understanding in the profoundest sense of the term. And for him, "To understand means to equal, to be capable of recreating all the stages which culminate in the work; it is believing that literature requires, at the outset, a specific attitude toward the subject and toward consciousness, a total vision of man as a 'structuring consciousness,' the recognition of the primacy of consciousness over the subconscious."[1]

One of the most significant ways in which this attitude reveals itself is through articles on individual authors, which date from very different times in his development and indicate the continuity of his evolution. In his early critical study devoted to Claudel's first plays, for example, Rivière sought to define the way in which Claudel's consciousness, as manifested in his plays, perceived the world. He emphasized the two-sided harmony of Claudel's dramatic vision and enthusiastically described the sense of awesome plenitude which his plays communicate to the reader. In a much later article on the stylistic difficulties of Claudel's dramatic and lyric poetry, Rivière reemphasized the metaphysical unity of Claudel's vision. And, in keeping with his own evolution, he was careful to point out the relationship he saw between certain of Claudel's concerns and those of the seventeenth-century French Classicists. He noted in particular how each of the elements in Claudel's creations forms part of a complex but carefully delineated aesthetic structure which reinforces the metaphysical harmony in his works.

Several years after his first article on Claudel, Rivière turned his attention to André Gide's works and sought to seize in Gide's creations a literary consciousness which was captivated by its own mobility. He demonstrated through numerous examples the cohesiveness of Gide's vision, but at the same time, he stressed the gradual change in attitude and focus which Gide's works revealed and analyzed the significance of that evolution in relation to his career as a whole. Rivière was encouraged by Gide's developing interest in his characters as individuals and by the growing mastery of narrative techniques which he saw manifested in Gide's *récits* in the first decade of the twentieth century. But Rivière became distressed when he saw that Gide did not go on to build upon these changes in his later works and because his vision seemed to remain static, rather than develop further in fullness and complexity.

When he confronted *A la Recherche du temps perdu* in the early 1920s, Rivière once again strove to define Proust's synthesizing quality and to demonstrate in specific terms how his masterpiece constituted a victory of consciousness over the subconscious. Proust examined the hidden recesses of the human psyche and made both startling and disconcerting discoveries concerning the nature of psychological motivation and the factors which influence it. As Rivière emphasized, Proust explored the layered complexity of the personality and explained it in precise detail through the creation of a work of art which, in turn, involves the reader's total personality and engages his complete emotional and intellectual attention.

Throughout his entire career, Rivière was influenced and inspired by many different kinds of writers from the time of his fascination with the Symbolist poets until the period when he championed Proust's cause. But it should again be stressed that he was never the disciple of anyone and never surrendered his own identity in literary explorations. As one of Rivière's contemporaries, the critic Benjamin Crémieux, notes in his reflections on Rivière's qualities: "On the one hand, there is in him, so quick to give of himself, an essential hardness or resistance to illusion, to fraud . . . and, on the other, a strong need not to reach the concrete directly, except by the detour of abstraction."[2]

On the one hand, it was the resistance of Rivière's own being, his certainty of his own reality, which made it possible for him to approach literary works as closely as he did without either distorting them or becoming lost in them himself. Rivière respected his own integrity too much to deny anyone else his independence. Despite his social timidity and the nervous anxiety that troubled him often, Rivière was also a tenacious fighter who rejected simplistic answers and who refused to give up even in the face of, at times, overwhelming opposition. As we have seen throughout our study, whether he was pursuing the childhood dream of a literary career as a young man, striving to take advantage of extremely adverse circumstances during the war, defining the *NRF* editorial policy, or insisting on the need for international cooperation, he would not yield to external pressure.

On the other hand, it was precisely his interest in abstract issues that inspired, for example, his pivotal theoretical study on the *roman d'aventure,* the essay which stands at the center of his literary concerns and further reveals the continuity of his evolution. It was as early as January 1905, while still an inexperienced schoolboy attracted to Symbolist poetry, that Rivière began to reveal his preoccupation with theoretical aesthetic issues that would assume such a significant position in his overall outlook for the rest of his life. In his very first letter to Fournier, Rivière described his reaction to the novel as it then existed, advocated reaffirmation of the ideals of French Classicism, and stressed the importance of the intellect as well as the emotions in the genesis of a truly satisfying work of art. The ideas outlined in this very early letter developed gradually over the years and were organized coherently and convincingly in his essay of 1913, "Le Roman d'aventure." During the war, Rivière became even more convinced that his convictions were correct concerning the general direction which literature should take. And in the early 1920s, his hopes for this kind of renewal came to rest on Proust, whose infinitely complex but precise work united scientific and aesthetic concerns, integrated the past and the present, and opened the door for other innovative forms of narrative investigation.

As we have seen, throughout his years as director of the *NRF* Rivière strove to make the review a truly international forum which welcomed contributors from many different countries and opposing points of view. He continued to emphasize his firm belief in the value of the Classical concept of literature which, without any moral preconceptions, explored even the most forbidden depths of the human personality in its quest for truth. And he stressed the importance of a modest, relative attitude, refusing to let literature become a quasi-sacred activity. But despite his personal preferences, Rivière also greeted other kinds of writing, such as many Surrealist creations, with tolerance and critical sensitivity, and he sought to understand the kind of torture which consumed the young Artaud. Like the music of *Le Sacre du printemps* or the atmosphere of the *roman d'aventure,* Rivière's own career was all action. He was caught up in the total adventure of living and describing the discoveries which he made within himself, in artistic creations, and in the world around him in precise terms which simultaneously reflect and clarify the complexity of his times.

Notes and References

Preface

1. Taine attempted to define what he believed were the laws governing literary creation, explaining all variables by the interaction of race, historical circumstances, and social milieu. Sainte-Beuve developed a more flexible, intuitive critical manner, but, in his desire to explain both literary works and then authors, he was limited by his biographical emphasis and also by the parallel he assumed existed between the author's presence in the work and his identity in real life.

2. This document was intended as a reply to Massis's attack on the novelist Raymond Radiguet, published in the 15 August 1924 issue of *La Revue universelle,* in which Massis ascribed to both Rivière and the *NRF* an attitude that was diametrically opposed to the reality of the situation.

3. Jacques Rivière, *Nouvelles Etudes* (Paris, 1947), p. 228. Many of Rivière's writings have been collected in the anthologies *Etudes* and *Nouvelles Etudes.* Each time we refer to an article which appears in one of these collections, we will indicate the source in the body of the text itself by using the abbreviations *E* and *NE* with the appropriate page number. The information pertaining to their specific date of publication will be presented in the bibliography. It should also be stressed that the translations of all the quotations are my own.

4. André Rivier, "Dix ans après. . . ," in *Jacques Rivière et ses amitiés suisses* (Lausanne, 1935), p. 134.

5. Ibid.

Chapter One

1. Helen L. Naughton, *Jacques Rivière, Development of a Man and a Creed* (Paris, 1966), p. 19.

2. Benjamin Crémieux, "Ce que n'était pas Rivière," *NRF* 24 (1925):488.

3. Naughton, *Jacques Rivière,* p. 20.

4. Jacques Rivière, "Méditation sur l'Extrême-Occident," *L'Occident* 12 (July 1907):20.

5. Ibid., p. 24.

6. Jacques Rivière, "Le Chemin de fer," *L'Occident* (April 1910), p. 157.

7. Jacques Rivière, "Les Beaux Jours," *NRF* 4 (1910):526.

8. Ibid., p. 528.

9. Jacques Rivière, "Histoire de Noé Sarambuca," *Mesures* 2 (1935):16.

10. Ibid., p. 19.

11. Ibid., p. 26.

12. Ibid., p. 24.

13. Henri Alban Fournier, who would adopt the literary name Henri Alain-Fournier, or simply Alain-Fournier, was the son of schoolteacher parents and came from the Sologne, a heavily forested, mysterious, and rather melancholy region of France just east of the Loire valley château country. Like Rivière, Fournier, too, had literary aspirations and would eventually publish one of the most huanting French novels ever written, entitled *Le Grand Meaulnes*.

14. In a highly autobiographical novel entitled *Un Bouquet de roses rouges*, published in 1935, Isabelle Rivière describes in detail the various stages of her own spiritual reawakening after her marriage and indicates as well the effect which her discoveries had on her husband.

Chapter Two

1. Jacques Rivière and Alain-Fournier, *Correspondance 1905–1914* (Paris, 1948), 1:8–9. (Subsequent references to volumes 1 and 2 of this work will be noted in the body of the text with the abbreviation *Corr. R-F, 1* or *2*, followed by the specific page number.)

2. Jacques Rivière, Introduction to *Miracles* (Paris, 1924), p. 18.

3. Henri de Règnier, *Tel qu'en songe*, as quoted in Rivière's introduction to *Miracles*, p. 17.

4. Claudel was one of the most powerful, most overwhelming French dramatists and poets, particularly for someone with Rivière's sensitive nature. His name is directly linked with Catholicism, for Claudel was not only an ardent believer himself, but also tried to bring others to accept the truths of the Catholic Church.

5. With respect to *Tête d'Or* Rivière remarks, "I had . . . the general feeling" (*Corr. R-F,* 1:155), while of *Les Muses*, he insists, "The entire beginning left me cold . . ." (*Corr. R-F* 1:155).

6. Jacques Rivière and Paul Claudel. *Correspondance 1907–1914* (Paris, 1926), pp. 77–78.

7. Concerning Rivière's reaction to the orthodoxy of Claudel's attitude, see his letters to Fournier dated 5 December 1906 and 23 December 1906.

8. Jacques Rivière, Letter to Gabriel Frizeau, 26 November 1907, in Paul Claudel et al., *Correspondance (1897–1938)* (Paris, 1952), p. 117.

9. Rivière and Claudel, *Correspondance,* p. 94.

10. Ibid., p. 101.

11. Paul Claudel, "Le Promeneur," in *Oeuvre poètique* (Paris: Gallimard, 1957), p. 84.

12. Ibid., p. 85.

13. Jacques Rivière, "Paul Claudel," *La Revue Rhénane,* no. 5 (February 1921), p. 238.

14. Ibid., p. 239.

15. Ibid., p. 236.

16. Ibid., p. 239.

17. See, for example, Rivière's comments to Fournier in the letters of 18 February 1907 and 20 April 1908, in which he describes his role-playing and explains how he was trying to bait Claudel with pantheistic statements inspired by the thesis he was then preparing on the seventeenth-century philosopher Fénelon.

18. Jacques Rivière, Letter to Gabriel Frizeau, 19 November 1907, in Claudel et al., *Correspondance,* p. 116.

Chapter Three

1. Even the eminent critic Henri Peyre refers to Rivière this way. See Henri Peyre, *Literature and Sincerity* (New Haven, 1963), p. 265.

2. André Gide, *Romans* (Paris: Gallimard, 1958), p. 248.

3. In order to be able to follow Rivière's evolution as closely as possible and to treat his relationship with Gide as thoroughly as it should be treated, it would be necessary to examine all the letters which the two men exchanged throughout Rivière's career. This voluminous correspondence has been edited by Professor Kevin O'Neill and is currently awaiting publication. Until the time when it is available, our knowledge of the rapport between the two men will be limited. Nevertheless, the few letters that Rivière wrote to Gide which have been published, the references made to Gide in Rivière's other published letters, and Gide's own comments about Rivière in some of his letters and in his journal do shed much light on the situation. And the information provided by Professor O'Neill's critical works dealing with

Gide and Rivière has also been very important in helping us to decipher at least the basic elements of a very complex relationship.

4. Jacques Rivière, "Lettres à André Gide," *NRF* 24 (1925):770.

5. Ibid., pp. 770–71.

6. The firest explanatory references to this proposed novel date from August 1908. Rivière worked as often as he could on this project over the next few years, making brief references to the work itself or to the revisions he was constantly planning (such as the title change to *Les Beaux Jours*) in his letters to Fournier, Frizeau, and Gide. By 1911, however, Rivière temporarily had to abandon the project altogether. In letters to Fournier from July 1911 onward, he still refers to "my book," but this time it is in relation to an anthology of critical articles which would be published under the title *Etudes*. As he explained in a letter to Claudel in August 1911, he fully intended to return to his novel, but his responsibilities at the *NRF* prevented him from working on it to any significant degree before the war. It was only during the years of his captivity that he would have the time to devote to a lengthy creative work, and, by that time, because of changes in his own life, the subject matter for the work would have altered completely from what it had been in *Les Beaux Jours*.

7. Rivière, "Lettres à Gide," p. 765.

8. Jacques Rivière, *De la Sincèritè envers soi-même* (Paris, 1943), p. 22.

9. Ibid., p. 31.

10. Ibid., p. 32.

11. Ibid., p. 34.

12. The problem of Gide's dedication to the cult of sincerity is too complex and far removed from Rivière for us to deal with it in this study. One of the clearest treatments of the whole issue appears in Henri Peyre's work entitled *Literature and Sincerity* (New Haven, 1963). It is sufficient for our purposes to stress that, although he was influenced by Gide's attitudes, Rivière thought in no way the same as Gide did about sincerity. Rivière's concern with personal sincerity troubled him long before he knew Gide, and his rejection of the doctrine of absolute sincerity is one of the many ways in which he asserted his independence from Gide.

13. Jacques Rivière, "De la Foi," in his *De la Sincérité envers soi-même* (Paris, 1943), p. 46.

14. Ibid., p. 68.

15. Ibid., p. 70.

16. Ibid., p. 93.

17. Rivière, "Lettres à Gide," p. 773.

18. Ibid., p. 777.

19. Ibid.

20. André Gide, "Jacques Rivière," *NRF* 24 (1925):499.

21. Rivière, "Lettres à Gide," pp. 776–77.

22. Henri Peyre, "Jacques Rivière and the Pursuit of Truth," *L'Esprit Créateur* 14, no. 2 (Summer 1974):113.

23. Maurice Nadeau, Introduction to André Gide, *Romans* (Paris: Gallimard, 1958), pp. 22–23.

24. The term *récit* in Gide's repertoire refers to a relatively short narrative that concentrates on the psychological evolution of a single major character and is usually told as a flashback.

25. Gide, *Romans,* p. 595.

26. Rivière, *De la Sincérité,* p. 22.

27. Kevin O'Neill, *André Gide and the Roman d'Aventure* (Sydney, 1969), p. 36.

28. Ibid.

29. Jacques Rivière, "André Gide," Part 1, *Chroniques des Lettres Françaises* 4 (January-February 1926):165.

30. We will again refer to Gide's attitude toward *Les Caves du Vatican* in the following chapter when we deal with Rivière's article on the evolution of the novel entitled "Le Roman d'aventure."

31. Rivière, "André Gide," p. 167.

32. Ibid.

33. Ibid., p. 168.

34. Ibid.

35. André Gide, *Morceaux choisis*, in Jacques Rivière, "André Gide," Part 2, *Chroniques des Lettres Françaises* 4 (May-June 1926):296.

36. Ibid., p. 300.

37. Ibid., p. 302.

38. Kevin O'Neill, "Jacques Rivière et André Gide: deux épisodes dans l'histoire de leurs relations (1920–1921)," in *Cahiers du 20ᵉ siècle,* no. 3 (Paris, 1975), pp. 28–47.

Chapter Four

1. The first issue of the *NRF* really came out 15 November 1908, but because of serious internal controversy concerning editorial policy, the goals had to be much more clearly defined and the editorial staff reorganized before it could resume publication.

2. Auguste Anglès, *André Gide et le premier groupe de La Nouvelle Revue Française* (Paris, 1978), p. 111.

3. See, for example, Claudel's comments in his letters to Rivière dated 8 and 12 October 1912 in which he expresses his indignation over the amoral attitude of the *NRF*'s editors.

4. As Auguste Anglès stresses in his treatise on the origins of the *NRF*, "For the first time in his life, his animation is not that of a connoisseur or a creator, but of a man of action" (Anglès, *André Gide et le premier groupe,* p. 161). It is also important to consider this remark in relation to Rivière's 1911 article on Gide, in which he pinpoints the same kind of evolution occurring in Gide's literary works dating from the same period—roughly 1905 onward. This comment by Anglès further substantiates the accuracy of Rivière's evaluation.

5. Jean Schlumberger, "Considérations," *NRF* 1 (1909):9–10.

6. For a very clear, succinct explanation of the *NRF*'s attitude toward the artist, see Rivière's article "À Propos, d'un Livre sur l'esthétique," *NRF* 8 (1912):545–47.

7. Albert Léonard, *La Crise du concept de littérature en France au XXe siècle* (Paris, 1974), p. 42.

8. Jacques Rivière and Paul Claudel. *Correspondance 1907–1914* (Paris, 1926), p. 142.

9. Anglès, *André Gide et le premier groupe,* p. 146.

10. Ibid., p. 233.

11. Ibid., p. 266.

12. Ibid., p. 267.

13. Jacques Rivière, *Quelques progrès dans l'étude du coeur humain (Freud et Proust)* (Paris, 1926), p. 113.

14. Pierre de Lanux had originally been Gide's personal secretary, and, beginning in June 1910, he also took over the position of secretary for the *NRF*. But when it became obvious that he lacked both the enthusiasm and the meticulousness needed for the post, he was relieved of his duties.

15. Lina Morino, *La Nouvelle Revue Française dans l'histoire des lettres* (Paris, 1939), pp. 65–66. Although Morino's book is both very general and superficial in comparison with Anglès's minutely detailed, scholarly study, it is nevertheless significant that, like Anglès, this critic, too, stresses Rivière's importance during even the early days of the *NRF*.

16. As it is used in this title, the term *métaphysique* seems to refer to the same effort to grasp, comprehend, and represent the mysterious or the unknown that Rivière had described in "Méditation sur l'Extrême-Occident." In his somewhat later essay on dreams, however,

the word does not have the specifically religious connotation it had in the earlier article. (See pages 22–23 of "Méditation sur l'Extrême-Occident," where Rivière explains in detail his conception of the term.)

17. Jacques Rivière, "Introduction à une Métaphysique du rêve," *NRF* 2 (1909):253.

18. Ibid., p. 251.

19. Ibid., p. 253.

20. Marcel Raymond, *De Baudelaire au surréalisme* (Paris: José Corti, 1969), p. 220.

21. Jacques Rivière, Letter to Gabriel Frizeau, 19 November 1907, in Paul Claudel et al., *Correspondance 1897–1938* (Paris, 1952), p. 115.

22. Ibid.

23. Rivière, "Méditation sur l'Extrême-Occident," p. 24.

24. As with Rivière's articles on painters, we shall concentrate on those which most clearly reveal the different stages in his development and are most closely related to his specifically literary evolution.

25. See, for example, Rivière's articles entitled "Le Sacre du printemps," and "Le Roman d'aventure."

26. Marcel Raymond, *Etudes sur Jacques Rivière* (Paris, 1972), pp. 171–74.

27. Kevin O'Neill notes in his introductory chapter that French interest in a *roman d'aventures* began with the critic Marcel Schwob in the early 1890s.

28. O'Neill, *André Gide,* pp. 24–25.

29. Ibid., p. 46.

30. Ibid., p. 54.

31. Raymond, *Etudes sur Jacques Rivière,* p. 183.

32. A great amount of heated controversy has surrounded the publication of Rivière's work on Rimbaud. The text, as published in 1930 by Rivière's widow, is the one which Rivière had prepared before World War I. A number of critics openly objected in the pages of the *NRF* to the work because of its narrow and strictly religious interpretation. They said, for example, that Rivière, who was so suspicious of easy solutions, would *never* have written the conclusion which appeared in the 1930 version, implying that his text had been tampered with. This kind of comment caused Isabelle Rivière ro react with equal outrage, insisting that the ending to the published text was definitely the ending that her husband had written in 1914 and proving her point with quotes from the working manuscript. Be that as it may, the relationship between the published text and Rivière's postwar attitudes still remains an important issue, especially in the light of a letter which Rivière

wrote to the critic Ernest-Robert Curtius in December 1923 and which the latter sent to the *NRF* at the time the Rimbaud controversy surfaced in the early 1930s. In his letter to Curtius, Rivière insisted on his profound change of opinion concerning his prewar Rimbaud study: " 'After the war I found myself in a completely different state of mind with respect to this article . . . I began to doubt the interpretation of *The Illuminations* which I had first constructed; their mystical character ceased to impress me. That is why I left my article unfinished. I will perhaps take it up again one day, redoing it completely' " (Jacques Rivière, Letter to E. R. Curtius, in E. R. Curtius, "Sur Rimbaud," *NRF* 37 [1931]:832). In the light of this kind of statement from Rivière himself, it seems accurate to say that even though the published Rimbaud study conforms to the manuscript, Rivière had, to a great extent, rejected the manuscript itself on his return from captivity. Although the text which Isabelle Rivière published is not a falsification, the interpretation of Rimbaud presented in the work seems to run counter to what Rivière would have written had he been able to pursue the Rimbaud project after the war.

33. Jacques Rivière, *Rimbaud* (Paris, 1930), p. 33.

34. Ibid., p. 106.

35. Ibid., p. 135.

36. Ibid., p. 177.

37. See Rivière's article "Baudelaire," *NRF* 4 (1910):721–40, later included in *Etudes*.

38. Rivière, *Rimbaud,* p. 234.

39. For a detailed discussion of the role of Rimbaud's poetry in Rivière's spiritual development and the evolution of Rivière's attitude toward Rimbaud, see the article by Roger Lefèvre, "Rivière lecteur de Rimbaud," in *Cahiers du 20ᵉ siècle,* no. 3 (Paris, 1975), pp. 49–64, and, even more importantly, his presentation and analysis of Rivière's complete repertoire of Rimbaud material entitled *Rimbaud Dossier 1905–1925* (Paris, 1977).

Chapter Five

1. The complete edition of Rivière's *Carnets* is divided into two principal sections, a short *Carnet de Guerre* dealing with the early weeks of his military experience before and immediately following his capture and the fourteen individual prison notebooks dating from 18 September 1914 to 23 May 1917.

2. Rivière was writing for himself with no thought concerning the effect he might be having on an audience, and the fact that he used

the term "notebooks" rather than "journal" to describe his entries further stresses the informality of the entries and their lack of literary pretentions.

3. Alain Rivière, Avertissement in Jacques Rivière, *Carnets* (Paris, 1974), p. xi. (All future references to Rivière's *Carnets* will be made in the text itself using the abbreviation *C* and the appropriate page number.)

4. The identity of Yvonne is suggested through Rivière's comments concerning her in his *Carnets* and through certain of Isabelle Rivière's explanatory notes.

5. Jacques Rivière, *A la Trace de Dieu* (Paris, 1925), p. 47.

6. Although the manuscript Rivière wrote in captivity is the first version of *Aimée,* he had conceived the project even before the war began. See Isabelle Rivière's preface to her husband's second, unfinished, novel, *Florence,* published in 1935.

7. See the correspondence exchanged between Rivière and Proust in 1921–22 for specific information concerning Rivière's progress with reworking *Aimée.*

8. See footnote 4 to the seventh notebook, where Isabelle Rivière describes in detail the organization of these special camps.

9. See, for example, his entry dated 23 December 1915 and the accompanying notes.

10. Jacques Rivière, *Aimée* (Paris, 1922), p. 13.

11. Ibid., p. 71.

12. See footnote 3 to the third notebook, where Isabelle Rivière describes her husband's attitude toward pity.

13. Rivière, *Aimée,* p. 208.

14. Ibid., p. 210.

15. Ibid., pp. 212–15.

16. Ibid., p. 219.

17. Ibid., p. 222.

18. Charles Du Bos, *"Aimée* par Jacques Rivière," *NRF* 20 (1923):158.

19. Jacques Rivière, *L'Allemand, Souvenirs et réflexions d'un prisonnier de guerre* (Paris, 1924), p. 21.

20. Jacques Rivière, *Le Français* (Paris, 1928), p. 131.

21. Jacques Rivière, "Pour une Société des Nations (1917–1918)," in *Cahiers de la Quinzaine, Cahier 14,* 19th ser. (Paris, 1930), p. 53.

22. Ibid., p. 50.

23. Ibid., p. 57.

24. See Rivière's angry letter "Contre une Société des Nations," written in March 1918 and published along with his essay in favor of forming a League of Nations.

25. Jacques Rivière, as quoted in Jacques Copeau, "Souvenirs d'un ami," *NRF* 24 (1925):437.

26. Jacques Rivière, "Letter to Mademoiselle Marie Fernaud," 12 August 1917, in *Jacques Rivière et ses amitiés suisses* (Lausanne, 1935), p. 15.

27. Ibid.

28. Ibid.

29. Alexis François, "Les Conférences de Jacques Rivière," in *Jacques Rivière et ses amitiés suisses,* p. 40.

30. Jacques Rivière, Letter to Alexis François, 23 February 1918, in *Jacques Rivière et ses amitiés suisses,* p. 41.

31. Paul Beaulieu, *Jacques Rivière* (Paris, 1956), p. 151.

Chapter Six

1. Jacques Rivière, Letter to Jean Schlumberger, 28 December 1916, in "Pour une reprise de *La Nouvelle Revue Française,*" *NRF* 45 (1975):20.

2. André Gide, Letter to Jacques Rivière, in "Pour une reprise," p. 21.

3. Jacques Rivière, Letter to Jean Schlumberger, 2 September 1917, in "Pour une reprise," p. 23.

4. Jean Schlumberger, *Oeuvres* (Paris: Gallimard, 1968), 2:197.

5. Ibid.

6. Jacques Rivière, Letter to Isabelle Rivière, 28 November 1918, in "Pour une reprise," p. 29.

7. Michel Arnauld, "Explications," *NRF* 13 (1919):209.

8. Ibid., p. 211.

9. Lina Morino, *La Nouvelle Revue Française dans l'histoire des lettres,* p. 113.

10. Jean Schlumberger, "Sur Le Parti de l'Intelligence," *NRF* 13 (1919):788.

11. Jacques Rivière, "Catholicisme et nationalisme," *NRF* 13 (1919):965.

12. Jacques Rivière, Letter to Isabelle Rivière, 28 November 1918, in "Pour une reprise," pp. 30–31.

13. In 1918 Gide's wife, Madeleine, discovered the full truth concerning her husband's homosexual relationships and burned all of the

letters that Gide had sent her over the years. Gide, for his part, believed that his letters to Madeleine expressed his purest and loftiest sentiments; he felt that she had destroyed the noblest part of his being when she destroyed them.

14. André Gide, Letter to Jacques Rivière, 21 August 1920, in Kevin O'Neill, "Jacques Rivière et André Gide: deux épisodes dans l'histoire de leurs relations, 1920–1921," *Cahiers du 20ᵉ siècle,* no. 3 (Paris, 1975), p. 33.

15. Ibid., p. 45.

16. Ibid., p. 46.

17. Ibid., p. 26.

18. André Gide, Letter to Marcel Proust, in Richard Barker, *Marcel Proust* (New York: Grosset and Dunlap, 1962), p. 222.

19. Kevin O'Neill, *André Gide and the Roman d'Aventure* (Sydney, 1969), p. 73.

20. Marcel Proust and Jacques Rivière, *Correspondance (1914–1922),* ed. Philip Kolb (Paris, 1955), p. 1.

21. Ibid., p. vii.

22. See, for example, the letters from July 1920, centered around the comments of the frequent *NRF* contributor Roger Allard.

23. The Prix Blumenthal was given by the American Foundation for French Art and Thought, an organization founded by Mrs. George Blumenthal, and brought a stipend of six thousand francs. See Proust's letter to Rivière dated 17 August 1920.

24. See Rivière's interview with Frédéric Lefèvre entitled *Une Heure avec . . .* , 2nd ser. (Paris, 1924). In this discussion, Rivière himself explains the relationship he could now discern between his prewar article and Proust's creation.

25. Jacques Rivière, *Quelques progrès dans l'étude du coeur humain (Freud et Proust)* (Paris, 1926), p. 11.

26. Ibid., p. 12.

27. Ibid., p. 18.

28. Ibid., p. 22.

29. Ibid., p. 33.

30. Ibid., p. 44.

31. Ibid., p. 53.

32. Ibid., p. 68.

33. Ibid., p. 81.

34. Ibid., p. 84.

35. Ibid., p. 118.

36. Jacques Rivière et Ramon Fernandez, *Moralisme et littérature* (Paris, 1932), p. 31.

37. Ibid., p. 37.

38. Ibid., p. 50.

39. Ibid., p. 83.

40. Ibid., p. 87.

41. Ibid., p. 101.

42. Ibid., p. 129.

43. Ibid., p. 122.

44. Ibid., p. 140.

45. Ibid., p. 147.

46. Ibid., p. 150.

47. It should be noted in defense of Rivière's openness as director, however, that despite his lack of personal enthusiasm for the artists who exhibited their works in the Salon des Indépendants, he nevertheless defended their right to do so. See his brief article entitled "L'Institut contre les Indépendants," which appeared in the July 1919 issue of the *NRF* and was included in *Nouvelles Etudes.*

48. Michel Décaudin, "Rivière et Dada," *Cahiers du 20ᵉ siècle,* no. 3 (Paris, 1975), p. 79.

49. For a more detailed explanation, see Kevin O'Neill's "Jacques Rivière et André Gide," pp. 29–32.

50. André Gide, "Dada," *NRF* 14 (1920):481.

51. Décaudin, "Rivière et Dada," p. 83.

52. Ibid.

53. See, for example, the exchange of letters between Rivière and Claudel from August and October 1922, in which Rivière defends a text by Louis Aragon that the *NRF* had published. The letters are published as part of the article "Pour une reprise de la *Nouvelle Revue Française,*" *NRF* 45 (1975).

54. Marcel Arland, "Pour un nouveau mal du siècle," *NRF* 22 (1924):157.

55. Maurice Blanchot, *Le Livre à venir* (Paris, 1959), p. 53.

56. Bettina Knapp, *Antonin Artaud, Man of Vision* (New York: David Lewis Inc., 1969), pp. 9–10.

57. Antonin Artaud, Letter to Jacques Rivière, 5 June 1923, in *Oeuvres complètes* (Paris: Gallimard, 1956), 1:20.

58. Jacques Rivière, Letter to Antonin Artaud, 23 June 1923, in Artaud, *Oeuvres,* p. 23.

59. Antonin Artaud, Letter to Jacques Rivière, 29 January 1924, in *Oeuvres,* p. 25.

60. Jacques Rivière, Letter to Antonin Artaud, 25 March 1924, in Artaud, *Oeuvres,* pp. 32–33.

61. Antonin Artaud, Letter to Jacques Rivière, 25 May 1924, in *Oeuvres,* p. 39.

62. Ibid.

63. Jacques Rivière, Letter to Antonin Artaud, 8 June 1924, in Artaud, *Oeuvres,* p. 43.

64. Ibid., p. 44.

65. Naomi Greene, *Antonin Artaud, Poet without Words* (New York, 1970), p. 65.

66. Jacques Rivière, Letter to Antonin Artaud, in Artaud, *Oeuvres,* p. 46.

67. The manuscript was eventually published in its unfinished state in 1935, and, like Rivière's earlier attempt with this genre, *Florence* is a static psychological analysis. Isabelle Rivière waited ten years before giving it to a publishing firm because of a request that her husband had made on his deathbed. He specifically asked her not to publish it, at least not until after everything else, because he did not want people to judge his own life according to the drama of sexual pursuit described in the work.

Florence depicts the relationship which develops between an extremely timid, egotistical, and overly intellectual young man named Pierre and an equally selfish but totally non-intellectual married woman who lives primarily for sensual pleasure. After a lengthy series of somewhat repetitious incidents, Pierre eventually comes to recognize the extent of Florence's hypocrisy and the depth of his own selfishness.

The work ends abruptly with a dialogue between two aspects of Pierre's personality meditating on his treatment of Florence and, even more importantly, on his relationship with God. But despite the hints of renewed spiritual awareness which are suggested in the last pages, we can only speculate as to the ultimate form the conclusion would have taken if Rivière had lived to complete the work.

Chapter Seven

1. Albert Léonard, *La Crise du concept de littérature en France au 20ᵉ siècle,* p. 186.

2. Benjamin Crémieux, "Ce que n'était pas Rivière," *NRF* 24 (1925):493.

Selected Bibliography

PRIMARY SOURCES

Listed in order of publication; abbreviations used: *NRF* for *Nouvelle Revue Française,* LZ for *Luxemburger Zeitung.* For a more complete bibliography see *Cahiers du 20ᵉ siècle* and H. T. Naughton's book on Rivière.

1. Books

Etudes. Paris: Gallimard, 1911.

L'Allemand, Souvenirs et réflexions d'un prisonnier de guerre. Paris: 1918. New edition with introduction, 1924.

Aimée. Paris: Gallimard, 1922.

Marcel Proust. (Société des Conférences, No. 5.) Monaco: Imprimerie de Monaco, 1924.

A la Trace de Dieu. Preface by Paul Claudel. Paris: Gallimard, 1925.

Quelques progrès dans l'étude du coeur humain (Freud et Proust). Paris: Libraire de France, 1926.

Carnet de guerre, août-septembre, 1914. Paris: Editions de la Belle Page, 1929.

Le Français. Paris: Editions Claude Aveline, 1928.

Pour et contre une Société des Nations (1917–1918). Cahiers de la Quinzaine. No. 14, 19th ser. Paris: Artisan du livre, 1930.

Rimbaud. Paris: Kra, 1930.

Moralisme et littérature. With Ramon Fernandez. Preface by Ramon Fernandez. Paris: Corrêa, 1935.

Florence. Introduction by Isabelle Rivière. Paris: Corrêa, 1935.

De la Sincérité envers soi-même, followed by "De la Foi," and "Chasse à l'orgueil." Introduction by Isabelle Rivière. Paris: Gallimard, 1943.

Nouvelles Etudes. Paris: Gallimard, 1947.

Carnets. Preface by Pierre Emmanuel. Introduction by Alain Rivière. Paris: Librairie Anthême, 1974.

2. Correspondence

Artaud, Antonin, and Rivière, Jacques. "Une Correspondance." *NRF* 23 (1924):291–312. Later published in Artaud, Antonin. *Oeuvres complètes*. Vol. 1. Paris: Gallimard, 1956.

Rivière-Gide. Lettres à André Gide. *NRF* 24 (1925):758–80.

Rivière, Jacques, and Claudel, Paul. *Correspondance 1907–1914*. Paris: Plon, 1926.

Rivière, Jacques, and Alain-Fournier. *Correspondance 1905–1914*. 4 vols. Paris: Gallimard, 1926. New edition in 2 vols. Paris: Gallimard, 1948.

Rivière, Jacques. Five letters to François Mauriac. In Mauriac, François. *Du Côté de chez Proust*. Paris: La Table Ronde, 1947.

Rivière, Jacques. Eleven letters to Gabriel Frizeau. In Claudel, Paul, et al. *Correspondance (1897–1938)*. Paris: Gallimard, 1952.

Proust, Marcel, and Rivière, Jacques. *Correspondance, 1914–1922*. Edited by Philip Kolb. Paris: Plon, 1955.

3. Articles in Periodicals

"Les Concerts." *Mercure Musical* (1906), pp. 430–33.

"Concerts." *Mercure Musical* (1906), p. 477.

"Concert Pugno-Ysaye." *Mercure Musical* (1906), pp. 530–31.

"La Saison théâtrale." *Mercure Musical* (1906), pp. 34–38.

"Notes sur le 23ᵉ Salon des Artistes Indépendants." *Tanit* 1 (1907):167–71.

"La Musique à Paris." *Tanit* 2 (1907):219–23.

"Méditation sur l'Extrême-Occident." *L'Occident* 12 (July 1907):19–25.

"Paul Claudel. Poète Chrétien" *L'Occident* 12 (October, November, December 1907):158–76, 210–20, 267–75.

"La Théodicée de Fénelon: Les éléments quiétistes." *Annales de Philosophie Chrétienne* 7, 80th year, 4th series (1908):113–47, 267–86; (1909):388–404, 502–15, 578–605.

"*Bouclier du Zodiaque* par André Suarès." *NRF* 1 (1909):260–64.

"André Lhote." *NRF* 1 (1909):293–94.

"Introduction à une Métaphysique du rêve." *NRF* 2 (1909):250–57.

"Pensée sur Chopin." *L'Occident* 12 (December 1909):249–51.

"*Dardanus* de Rameau à la Schola Cantorum." *NRF* 2 (1909):552–54.

"Festival Franck aux concerts Colonne." *NRF* 3 (1910):129–31.

"*Claude Debussy,* par L. Laloy." *NRF* 3 (1910):131–33.

"*La Rhapsodie espagnole* de Ravel aux Concerts Colonne." *NRF* 3 (1910):134–35.

"Sur la Mort de l'aviateur Delagrange." *NRF* 3 (1910):135–36.

"Cézanne." *NRF* 3 (1910):366–70.

"Le Chemin de fer." *L'Occident,* April 1910, pp. 151–59.

"Les Poèmes d'orchestre de Claude Debussy." *NRF* 3 (1910):476–82.

"Exposition Henri Matisse." *NRF* 3 (1910):531–34.

"Exposition Georges Rouault." *NRF* 3 (1910):537–38.

"*La Passion selon Saint-Jean* de Bach." NRF 3 (1910):538–41.

"*Deux poèmes pour chant et orchestre* de Florent Schmitt." *NRF* 3 (1910):541.

"Albert Besnard, décorateur." *Art et Décoration,* 27 May 1910, pp. 153–70.

"*Ariane et Barbe-Bleue* de Paul Dukas à l'Opéra Comique." *NRF* 3 (1910):686–89.

"Paul Gauguin." *NRF* 3 (1910):738–43.

"Voyage à Reims." *NRF* 4 (1910):169–75.

"Les Oeuvres lyriques de Claudel." *Art Libre* 10 (1910):361–66.

"Les Beaux Jours." *NRF* 4 (1910):521–30.

"Baudelaire." *NRF* 4 (1910):721–40.

"Exposition H. E. Cross." *NRF* 4 (1910):805–806.

"Exposition André Lhote." *NRF* 4 (1910):806–808.

"Sur le *Tristan et Isolde* de Wagner." *NRF* 5 (1911):29–33.

"Les Scènes Polovtsiennes du *Prince Igor* aux Concerts Colonne." *NRF* 5 (1911):172–73.

"Musorgski." *NRF* 5 (February 1911):314–17.

"Reprise de *Pelléas et Mélisande* à l'Opéra Comique." *NRF* 5 (1911):623–25.

"*Les Frères Karamazov* au Théâtre des Arts." *NRF* 5 (1911):757–60.

"Ingres." *NRF* 5 (1911):832–37.

"Expositions Maurice Denis et Pierre Bonnard." *NRF* 6 (1911):137–38.

"*Petrouchka,* ballet d'Igor Stravinski." *NRF* 6 (1911):376–77.

"*Théâtre* par Paul Claudel: I: *Tête d'Or* (première et seconde versions) II: *La Ville* (première et seconde versions)." *NRF* 6 (1911):477–82.

"André Gide." *La Grande Revue* 69 (October 1911):757–77; 70 (November 1911):90–112.

"De la Sincérité envers soi-même." *NRF* 7 (1912):5–18.

"A propos d'une prochaine exposition des Pompiers." *NRF* 7 (1912):118–19.

"Exposition de peintures chinoises." *NRF* 7 (1912):300–303.

"Les Ciels." *Art et Décoration* 29 (February 1912):47–59.

"Exposition Félix Vallotton." *NRF* 7 (1912):499–502.

"Oeuvres de piano de J. S. Bach." *NRF* 7 (1912):502–503.

"Poussin et la peinture contemporaine." *L'Art Décoratif* 27 (5 March 1912):133–48.

"Sur les tendances actuelles de la peinture." *Revue d'Europe et d'Amérique* (1912), pp. 383–406.

"Portrait de Joachim Du Bellay." *NRF* 7 (1912):519–22.

"Le Salon des Indépendants." *NRF* 7 (1912):890–93.

"Le Mystère des Saints Innocents de Péguy." *NRF* 7 (1912):980–86.

"Des Ballets Russes et de Fokine." *NRF* 8 (1912):174–80.

"La Peinture aux deux Salons." *Art et Décoration* 32 (July 1912):17–32.

"A Propos d'un Livre sur l'esthétique." *NRF* 8 (1912):545–47.

"De la Foi." *NRF* 8 (1912):780–809, 970–97.

"René Bichet." *NRF* 9 (1913):312–16.

"Jean-Arthur Rimbaud, le poète, par Paterne Berrichon." *NRF* 9 (1913):329–30.

"Le Roman d'aventure." *NRF* 9 (1913):748–65, 914–32; 10 (1913):56–77.

"Exposition de David et de ses élèves." *NRF* 9 (1913):841–45.

"Pénélope de Gabriel Fauré et *la Passion selon Saint Mathieu* de J. S. Bach aux Champs-Elysées." *NRF* 9 (1913):1037–40.

"Sur les Indépendants." *NRF* 9 (1913):1040–41.

"Le Sacre du printemps. Ballet par Igor Stravinsky, Nicolas Roerich, Vlaslav Nijinski. . . ." *NRF* 10 (1913):309–13.

"Le Sacre du printemps." NRF 10 (1913):706–30.

"Exposition Cézanne." *NRF* 11 (1914):351–52.

"Parsifal." NRF 11 (1914):757–69.

"Rimbaud." *NRF* 12 (1914):5–48, 209–30.

"La Saison russe." *NRF* 12 (1914):150–62.

"La Nouvelle Revue Française." *NRF* 13 (1919):1–12.

"Nos Morts: Emile Verhaeren, Charles Péguy, Alain-Fournier." *NRF* 13 (1919):144–45.

"Belphégor, par J. Benda." *NRF* 13 (1919):146–53.

"Notice sur Charles Péguy." *NRF* 13 (1919):161–62.

"L'Institut contre les Indépendants." *NRF* 13 (1919):316–17.

"La Décadence de la liberté." *NRF* 13 (1919):498–522.

"Le Parti de l'Intelligence." *NRF* 13 (1919):612–18.

"Catholicisme et nationalisme." *NRF* 13 (1919):965–68.

"Marcel Proust." *Excelsior.* December 11, 1919, p. 4.

"Le Prix Goncourt." *NRF* 14 (1920):152–54.

"Marcel Proust et la tradition classique." *NRF* 14 (1920):192–200.

"Les Ballets russes à l'Opéra: La Boutique fantasque, le Tricorne, le Chant du Rossignol." *NRF* 14 (1920):462–67.

"Reconnaissance à Dada." *NRF* 15 (1920):216–37.

"M. Pierre Lasserre contre Marcel Proust." *NRF* 15 (1920):481–83.

"La Surprise de l'amour de Marivaux, au Vieux Colombier." *NRF* 15 (1920):958–61.

"Note à propos de M. Eugène Montfort." *NRF* 16 (1921):512.

"Notes sur un événement politique." *NRF* 16 (1921):558–71.

"Le Héros et le soldat de Bernard Shaw. *Les Amants puérils* de F. Crommelynck." *NRF* 16 (1921):621–23.

"Le Choeur Ukrainien." *NRF* 16 (1921):626–27.

"M. Paul Souday et la politique." *NRF* 17 (1921):251–52.

"Les Lettres françaises et la guerre." *La Revue Rhénane* 2 (1921):860–69.

"Amiel." *NRF* 17 (1921):680–81.

"De Dostoievski et de l'insondable." *NRF* 18 (1922):175–78.

"Les Dangers d'une politique conséquente." *NRF* 19 (1922):5–11.

"Paul Valéry, poète." *NRF* 19 (1922):257–69.

Several pages of Aimée. *Les Nouvelles Littéraires,* 10th year, no. 2 (28 October 1922):2ff.

"La Chute de Lloyd George." *LZ,* November 1, 1922.

"Maurice Barrès et la critique catholique." *NRF* 19 (1922):621–25.

"Le Secret professionnel par Jean Cocteau." *NRF* 19 (1922):631–33.

"Les Lettres à Paris." *LZ,* December 2, 1922.

"Marcel Proust." *NRF* 19 (1922):641–42.

"Alain-Fournier." *NRF* 19 (1922):643–68; 20 (1923):374–94.

"La France et l'Allemagne." *LZ,* January 4, 1923.

"Marcel Proust et l'esprit positif." *NRF* 20 (1923):179–87.

"L'Occupation de la Ruhr." *LZ,* February 3, 1923.

"Comment en sortir." *LZ,* March 6, 1923.

"Les Obstacles aux négociations." *LZ,* April 4, 1923.

"Les Aventures de Télémaque, par Louis Aragon." *NRF* 20 (1923):700–703.

"Les Discours de Lord Curzon." *LZ,* May 3, 1923.

"Pour une Entente économique avec l'Allemagne." *NRF* 20 (1923):725–35.

"Les Offres de l'Allemagne." *LZ,* June 3, 1923.

"Répétitions." *LZ,* July 6, 1923.

"Le Fleuve de Feu par François Mauriac." *NRF* 21 (1923):98–101.

"La Politique de la raison pure." *LZ,* August 7, 1923.

"Un peu d'espoir." *LZ,* September 6, 1923.

"D'une Utilisation moderne de la victoire." *LZ,* October 8, 1923.

"L'Anniversaire de la mort de Marcel Proust." *NRF* 21 (1923):736.

"Retour à l'optimisme." *LZ,* Januray 6, 1924.

"La Fin d'une politique." *LZ,* February 9, 1924.

"La Crise du concept de littérature." *NRF* 22 (1924):159–70.

"Un nouveau Wilson." *LZ,* March 14, 1924.

"M. Jacques Rivière et les peintres." *Almanach des Lettres Françaises et Etrangères,* 1 (1924):322.

"Le nouveau Ministère Poincaré et les chances du règlement." *LZ,* April 17, 1924.

"La Situation est transformée." *LZ,* May 16, 1924.

"Le Bal du comte d'Orgel par Raymond Radiguet." *NRF* 22 (1924):692–93.

"La Paix est déclenchée." *LZ,* June 28, 1924.

"La Conférence de Londres et le véto des banquiers." *LZ,* August 6, 1924.

"Lettre ouverte à Henri Massis sur les bons et les mauvais sentiments." *NRF* 23 (1924):416–25.

"Le Problème de la sécurité." *LZ,* October 16, 1924.

"Le Triomphe des conservateurs en Angleterre." *LZ,* November 21, 1924.

"Notes sur le nationalisme allemand." *LZ,* December 24, 1924.

"Sur une généralisation possible des théories de Freud." *Le Disque Vert,* 2nd year, n.s. 3, 1924.

"Sur la prière." *La Revue Universelle* 20 (August 1925):159–69.

"André Gide." *Chronique des Lettres Françaises* 4 (1926):145–68, 289–303.

"22–25 août 1914." *Commerce* 8 (Summer 1926):169–204.

"En Marge de l'Allemand." *NRF* 30 (1928):289–97.

"Chasse à l'orgueil." *Vigile* 2ᵉ Cahier (1930):7–70.

"Progrès, Civilisation, Culture." *La Vie Intellectuelle* 2, no. 3 (1931):441–45.

"Russes." *La Vie Intellectuelle* 10, no. 3 (1931):484–509.

"Histoire de Noé Sarambuca." *Mesures* 2 (1935):13–28.

SECONDARY SOURCES

1. Books

Alain-Fournier. *Le Grand Meaulnes.* Paris: Editions Emile Paul, 1913. Fournier's haunting novel depicting the conflict between childhood and adolescence, the past and the future, the earth and the beyond.

————. *Miracles.* Introduction by Jacques Rivière. Paris: Gallimard, 1924. Series of poems, short stories, essays, and vignettes which introduce the themes developed in depth in *Le Grand Meaulnes.*

Anglès, Auguste. *André Gide et le premier groupe de La Nouvelle Revue Française. La formation du groupe et les années d'apprentissage 1890–1910.* Paris: Gallimard, 1978. Detailed and meticulously documented study of the *NRF*'s beginnings, containing important information on Rivière's role in the undertaking.

Beaulieu, Paul. *Jacques Rivière.* Paris: Editions du Vieux Colombier, 1956. A sensitive, fair, and critically sound discussion of Rivière's overall evolution.

Blanchot, Maurice. *Le Livre à venir.* Paris: Gallimard, 1959. A brilliant and provocative critical meditation which is indispensable for understanding the complexity of the relationship between the author and his work and that which exists between the text and the reader; contains an important section on Rivière and Artaud.

Charlot, Pierre. *Jacques Rivière, une vie ardente et sincère.* Paris: Bloud et Gay, 1934. An outdated text examining Rivière's evolution in general terms from a very restricted religious viewpoint.

Les Chemins actuels de la critique. Edited by Georges Poulet. Paris: Union Générale des Editions, 1963. Proceedings from the Cerisy colloquium on twnetieth-century French criticism. Poulet's opening remarks and the ensuing discussion contain significant references to Rivière's critical approach.

Cook Bradford. *Jacques Rivière: A Life of the Spirit.* Oxford: Basil Blackwell, 1958. An important work for understanding Rivière's spiritual development, but the discussion often becomes bogged down in religious rhetoric.

Greene, Naomi. *Antonin Artaud, Poet Without Words.* Introduction by Janet Flanner. New York: Simon and Schuster, 1970. A very perceptive analysis of Artaud's special dilemma in the context of twentieth-century literary developments.

Jacques Rivière et ses amitiés suisses. Lausanne: Faculté des Lettres de l'Université de Lausanne, 1935. An extremely valuable compendium of letters, critical essays, excerpts from speeches, etc. dating from Rivière's stay in Switzerland, which sheds much light on this little-known period of his career.

Lefèvre, Frédéric. *Une Heure avec . . .* 2nd ser. Paris: Nouvelle Revue Française, 1924. Extremely important interview highlighting Rivière's postwar critical ideas.

Lefèvre, Roger. *Rimbaud Dossier 1905–1925.* Paris: Gallimard, 1977. A minutely detailed and carefully organized compendium of all the documents that reveal the evolution in Rivière's attitude toward Rimbaud.

Léonard, Albert. *La Crise du concept de littérature en France au XXe siècle.* Paris: Librairie José Corti, 1974. Although the work as a whole is quite biased against recent developments in French criticism, it does, nonetheless, contain a perceptive discussion of Rivière's importance as a critic and director of the *NRF*.

Morino, Lina. *La Nouvelle Revue Française dans l'histoire des lettres.* Paris: Gallimard, 1939. A general, but nevertheless very valuable presentation of the importance of the *NRF* and of Rivière's role in its development.

Naughton, Helen T. *Jacques Rivière, The Development of a Man and a Creed.* Paris: Mouton and Co., 1966. A serious, well-documented study which is invaluable for understanding the intricacies of Rivière's literary, psychological, and spiritual evolution and his relationship with many of the important creative writers of early-twentieth-century France.

O'Neill, Kevin. *André Gide and the Roman d'Aventure.* Sydney: Sydney University Press, 1969. A most enlightening analysis of the importance of this complex phenomenon in Gide's evolution, of Rivière's position in relation to it, and of the conflict which arose between the two men over this issue.

————, et al. *Cahiers du 20e siècle.* No. 3. Paris: Klincksieck, 1975. An extremely valuable anthology of articles offering new insight into such important topics as Rivière and Rimbaud, Rivière and Claudel, Rivière and Proust, Rivière and Dada, Rivière and Gide after World War I.

Paré, Sylvie. "Jacques Rivière, Critique de Marcel Proust." Ph.D. Diss. University of Arizona, 1974. A precise, in-depth analysis of this aspect of Rivière's career, which, until this time, had been treated only in general terms.

Peyre, Henri. *Literature and Sincerity.* New Haven: Yale University Press, 1963. Important for understanding the similarities and differences between Gide's attitude toward sincerity and Rivière's.

Price, Blanche. *Jacques Rivière and His Literary Criticism.* Ann Arbor, Mich.: University Microfilms, 1953. One of the earliest serious studies which presents a carefully developed picture of the various stages of Rivière's evolution as a critic.

Raymond, Marcel. *Etudes sur Jacques Rivière.* Paris: Librairie José Corti, 1972. Incisive analysis of Rivière's critical development as revealed through the articles collected in *Etudes* and *Nouvelles Etudes.*

Rivière, Isabelle. *Le Bouquet de roses rouges.* Paris: Corrêa, 1936. Highly autobiographical novel describing the early years of her marriage and her religious conversion.

————, and Rivière, Jacques. *La Guérison.* Paris: Corrêa, 1936. A novel with strong autobiographical overtones which depicts the protagonist's experience as a prisoner of war and the way in which he worked out his psychological and spiritual difficulties.

Suffran, Michel. *Jacques Rivière et la conversion à la clarté.* Paris: Wesmail-Charlíer, 1967. A very limited and dogmatic study describing Rivière's development exclusively in terms of religious conversion.

Turnell, Martin. *Jacques Rivière.* (Studies in Modern European Literature and Thought.) New Haven: Yale University Press, 1953. A general, but well-done, introduction to Rivière and his works.

2. Articles in Periodicals

Arland, Marcel. "Sur un nouveau mal du siècle." *NRF* 22 (1924):149–58. Sensitive assessment of the malaise of the twentieth century; important for understanding Rivière's position.

Breton, André. "Pour Dada." *NRF* 14 (1920):208–15. Breton's apology for Dadaism, which is indispensable for appreciating Rivière's reaction to it.

Cap, Jean-Pierre. "Une amitié littéraire: Jacques Rivière–Jean Schlumberger." *Présence Francophone* 5 (1972):107–12. A perceptive evaluation of the intellectual relationship between the two men.

————. "Jean Schlumberger et *la Nouvelle Revue Française* 1909–1914." *L'Esprit Créateur* 14, no. 2 (Summer 1974):99–109. Valuable description of Schlumberger's role with the *NRF*.

Copeau, Jacques "Souvenirs d'un ami." *NRF* 24 (1925):434–42. Sensitive commemorative article by one of the *NRF* group whose friendship Rivière valued very highly.

Crémieux, Benjamin. "Ce que n'était pas Rivière." *NRF* 24 (1925):487–96. A commemorative article stressing Rivière's commitment to sincerity and perfection.

Curtius, E. R. "Sur Rimbaud." *NRF* 37 (1931):831–32. Important document in the controversy surrounding Rivière's attitude toward Rimbaud.

Du Bos, Charles. *Aimée* par Jacques Rivière." *NRF* 20 (1923):560–66. Very favorable review of Rivière's novel *Aimée;* seems to be inspired more by friendship than by critical conviction.

————. "Jacques Rivière et la perfection abstraite." *NRF* 24 (1925):580–88. Commemorative article singling out Rivière's theoretical mind and his exceptionally high critical standards.

Eustis, Alvin. "Rivière's Crew: Crémieux, Fernandez, Arland." *L'Esprit Créateur* 14 (Summer 1974):138–45. Very informative discussion of Rivière's years as *NRF* director and of his relationship with the other critics who wrote for the review.

Fernandez, Ramon. "In Memoriam." *NRF* 24 (1925):572–79. Commemorative article stressing Rivière's dedication to truth and perfection.

————. "Jacques Rivière et le moralisme." *NRF* 28 (1927):279–82. Fernandez's evaluation of Rivière's position on this issue; important because of their earlier debates.

Gide, André. "Dada." *NRF* 14 (1920):477–81. Gide's assessment of Dadaism; important for understanding Rivière's position.

————. "Billet à Angèle." *NRF* 16 (1921):462–66. Gide's letter seriously criticizing Rivière's running of the *NRF* and its editorial policies.

Naughton, Helen T. "Temperament and Creed. A Note on Jacques Rivière." *French Review* 36 (1963):471–81. Carefully thought out discussion of Rivière's commitment to truth.

————. "The Realism of Jacques Rivière." *Modern Language Quarterly* 25, no. 2 (June 1964):171–80. Very informative discussion of Rivière's definition of the term "realism" and of the changes in his attitude toward it as he matured intellectually and emotionally.

————. "A Contemporary views Proust." *L'Esprit Créateur* 5, no. 1 (Spring 1965):48–55. Good introduction to this aspect of Rivière's criticism.

————. "The Critic's Cure: Rivière's *Aimée.*" *Renascence* 17, no. 4 (Summer 1965):201–206. Interpretative exploration of the relationships among Rivière's novel, his conception of the adventure novel, and his personal experiences.

Peyre, Henri. "Jacques Rivière and the Pursuit of Truth." *L'Esprit Créateur* 14, no. 2 (Summer 1974):110–20. A very sound, well-substantiated appraisal of Rivière's postwar critical repertoire emphasizing his fairness and openmindedness.

"Pour une reprise de *La Nouvelle Revue Française.*" *NRF* 45, no. 266 (1975):19–49. An invaluable series of documents (mainly letters from 1917–1925) revealing Rivière's attitude toward the directorship of the *NRF* and the direction he felt that the review should take.

Price, Blanche. "Jacques Rivière on *Moralisme et littérature.*" *French Review* 17, no. 4 (February 1944):214–19. Perceptive and well-documented discussion of Rivière's views on this subject and of the differences between him and Fernandez.

Raymond, Marcel. "Jacques Rivière devant l'histoire et les nationalités." *L'Esprit Créateur* 14, no. 2 (Summer 1974):121–37. Sensitive assessment of Rivière's political ideas; very helpful for understanding his postwar development.

Rivière, Alain. "Jacques Rivière et Marcel Proust." *Bulletin de la Société des amis de Marcel Proust et de Combray* 27 (1977):513–29. Very helpful article by Rivière's son offering new insights into his father's attitude toward Proust and the intellectual relationship between critic and novelist.

Rivière, Isabelle. "Lettre." *NRF* 26 (1926):602–609. Isabelle Rivière's response to what she believed were gross inaccuracies in certain of the commemorative articles dedicated to her husband and her justification for publishing *A la Trace de Dieu* first, before anything else, after her husband's death.

———. "The Miracle of Jacques Rivière." *Commonweal* 6, no. 2 (18 May 1927):40–42. Brief summary of Rivière's religious evolution and commitment to Catholicism.

———. "Rectification." *NRF* 37 (1931):333–35.

———. "Seconde rectification." *NRF* 37 (1931):610–20. Both of these articles help to clarify the terms of the controversy surrounding Rivière's attitude toward Rimbaud.

———. "Jacques Rivière et André Gide." *La Vie Intellectuelle* 21 (1933):280–306; 21 (1933):480–505. Clarification of some of the points of disagreement between the two men.

Rolland de Renéville, André. "*Arthur Rimbaud* par Jacques Rivière." *NRF* 37 (1931):144–48. Review of recent Rimbaud criticism, including Rivière's work, which he criticizes for what he feels is an added, specifically "Catholic" conclusion that falsifies Rivière's original interpretation, presented in the *NRF* in 1914.

Schlumberger, Jean. "Considérations." *NRF* 1 (1909):5–11. Manifesto of the *NRF*.

Turnell, Martin. "The Problem of Jacques Rivière." *Dublin Review* 199 (October 1936):385–98. Turnell's evaluation of Rivière's spiritual dilemma.

———. "A Note on Jacques Rivière." *Commonweal* 14 (1951):479–81. Very abridged assessment of Rivière's religious ideas in relation to his times.

Index